MW00986402

"James Levesque is an en
sure evidence that anothe
out. His insatiable appetit
zeal and vision for not just reading about the great things God
has done but experiencing them, fills the pages of this book.
This is lighter fluid for the coming fire of revival."

Rick Joyner, founder, MorningStar Ministries

"Fire always falls on sacrifice. In true worship, we are the sacrifice. As His royal priesthood, we steward the flames of His
presence by becoming the offering given for His glory. We've
been designed as a resting place for the Spirit of God, changing
every environment that we walk into. When James writes, 'On
earth as it is in heaven,' it is not just a Christian platitude. It is
our mandate, and it is attainable."

Bill Johnson, author, *The Way of Life* and *Raising Giant-
Killers*; senior leader, Bethel Church, Redding, California

"From the beginning of our ministry, God revealed to us that
prayer and intense intercession were a vital part of the spiritual
victory He would give us. I've learned since then that in order
to see revival we must humble ourselves before God's presence.
There is no time like the present to go and share the good news
to every creature. Signs will follow those who believe. Let's
move forward and pass the mantle to the next generation."

Carlos Annacondia, senior evangelist, International Message
of Salvation

"I have witnessed firsthand James Levesque's great love for the
Lord and his desire to see God's Kingdom manifested on earth
and people saved and set free. In *Fire!* James shares powerful
testimonies of God's intervention and relevant biblical truth of
how others can move in the supernatural dimension of God and
experience transforming personal encounters. It is my pleasure

to recommend this book, and I pray that it will greatly impact this generation for the present time and the days ahead."

Paul Keith Davis, founder, WhiteDove Ministries

"America is in desperate need of a massive spiritual awakening, but unless we are spiritually desperate, we will never experience the awakening we need. In this practical and passionate book, James Levesque calls us to pursue God afresh for the greatest revival our nation has ever seen, starting in each of our lives. It's time for a fresh encounter!"

Dr. Michael L. Brown, author, *From Holy Laughter to Holy Fire*; host, *The Line of Fire* radio broadcast

"James Levesque is a firebrand evangelist who walks the walk and talks the talk. His book will stir you, inspire you and thrust you forth, preparing you for the unprecedented revival that is about to fall on North America and the nations of this world. Allow James to coach you, lighting the fires of the Holy Spirit for revival and passion for Jesus. May these truths grip your heart like never before, as you prepare to fruitfully carry the fiery love and power of God."

John Arnott, founder, Catch The Fire, Toronto

"I have been part of James's life and ministry for several years. I endorse, I bless and I back the holy fire of the Lord God on this book!"

David Hogan, missionary, Freedom Ministries

"Jesus described Nathanael this way, 'Behold, an Israelite indeed, in whom is no guile.' Jesus was once described this way, 'Zeal for your house has eaten me up.' Both of these word pictures accurately describe James Levesque and his new book *Fire!* He is a man who has been consumed with not just a longing for revival in New England but a zeal for the full restoration of the Body of Christ. The world needs more James Levesques."

Robin McMillan, senior pastor, Queen City Church, Charlotte, North Carolina

"There are very few voices today that carry the fire of God like my friend Pastor James Levesque! Not only is James a walking miracle, but he experiences miracles wherever he goes. *Fire!* will stoke the flames of revival in your life. It will force you to 're-move the filter' that you have placed on Jesus. This book will be read by generations to come as a guide to living a supernatural life. Share this book! For our God truly is 'a consuming fire' (Hebrews 12:29)."

Pat Schatzline, author and international evangelist, Remnant Ministries International

"If the call to imitate Jesus becomes your passion, He will show you how so that His glory may be revealed. Let the message of this book make you thirsty for what only the Holy Spirit can produce and hungry for what only the Word of God can awaken you to be."

Mark Spitsbergen, pastor, Abiding Place Ministry, San Diego, California

"This timely book by James Levesque is much needed for this generation, in a time when seeker-sensitive and politically correct preachers abound. Jesus is the Baptizer in the Holy Ghost and fire. This fire is for a purpose—I highly recommend this book."

Dr. Rodney Howard-Browne, Revival Ministries International, Tampa, Florida

FIRE!

PREPARING FOR THE NEXT GREAT
HOLY SPIRIT OUTPOURING

JAMES LEVESQUE

Chosen

a division of Baker Publishing Group
Minneapolis, Minnesota

© 2019 by James Levesque

Published by Chosen Books
11400 Hampshire Avenue South
Bloomington, Minnesota 55438
www.chosenbooks.com

Chosen Books is a division of
Baker Publishing Group, Grand Rapids, Michigan

Printed in the United States of America

Library of Congress Cataloging-in-Publication Data
Names: Levesque, James, author.
Title: Fire! : preparing for the next great Holy Spirit outpouring / James Levesque.
Description: Minneapolis : Chosen, a division of Baker Publishing Group, 2019.
Identifiers: LCCN 2018053759| ISBN 9780800799335 (trade paper : alk. paper)
    |ISBN 9781493418879 (e-book)
Subjects: LCSH: Religious awakening. | Revivals.
Classification: LCC BV3790 .L38 2019 | DDC 269—dc23
LC record available athttps://lccn.loc.gov/2018053759

In keeping with biblical principles of creation stewardship, Baker Publishing Group advocates the responsible use of our natural resources. As a member of the Green Press Initiative, our company uses recycled paper when possible. The text paper of this book is composed in part of post-consumer waste.

Cover design by Rob Williams, InsideOutCreativeArts

20 21 22 23 24 25 26   8 7 6 5 4 3 2

green
press
INITIATIVE

I would like to dedicate this book to two groups of people:

To the men and women of the First and Second Great
Awakenings. Your passion and pursuit of God are
contagious and continue to transform this world
today. Thank you for preaching and proclaiming
the message of the Gospel with boldness.

To my daughter, Amayah,
and to my sons, Isaac and Luke,
who, should the Lord tarry, will carry this message
and continue carrying this fire into their generation.

Contents

Foreword

God has a wonderful plan for your life. It is a plan to make you into a fiery messenger of Jesus Christ! You were not meant for status-quo Christianity. Something is already kindled in your heart, and it is called passion for God! Yes, He has a plan to make you more passionate, more fiery than you want to be.

How can we love God and serve Him without fire, for our God is an endless flame, a consuming fire? Today's church culture needs an upgrade. We need every believer to be activated, encouraged and flowing in the river of God. Imagine how the world will change around us when believers catch on fire! The Word of God is there to light the spark. The Holy Spirit is present and ready to fan it into a flame. And our holy passion for Jesus will be the fire!

Have we forgotten that the church was born in the flames of Pentecost, with flames of fire resting upon each believer? I love how James Levesque says it:

"Years ago, fire was understood and talked about. Today we run from it. I believe that this lack of understanding of fire has contributed to the lukewarm Christian climate we are currently living in. If we don't want to be dying flames, we need to know more about the fire of God."

I have had the joy of being a part of James's incredible journey into heaven's living flames. I have watched in awe at times of the supernatural grace God has imparted to James Levesque. We were once together in Saint John, New Brunswick, at a wonderful conference. The fire that James writes about fell upon all who were in that meeting! It was amazing and frightful at the same time. Both James and I hit the deck as waves of heaven's glory washed over us. Barely able to move, we crawled closer to the altar and invited everyone to take all they could receive of God's presence. I love being with James, for he carries revival fire. Yes, God has His hand on the life of James Levesque. God is filling His people today, and He is shaping us into vessels who can carry the fire of God's Spirit. People with character, virtue and passion for God.

I have not read a book like this for many years. It stirred me as I turned each page. Something was reignited in my heart. I can testify that God's presence is released through the words of *Fire!* Rarely have I read a book that moved me as deeply as reading this one. You, too, will become a different person. Read it carefully. Underline the parts that speak powerfully to you. It is a brilliant exposition of revival and what God wants from our hearts today. Oh, make sure you read James's glorious encounter with God's fire that he shares in the introduction, so don't skip over it! And make sure you get a copy or two of the book to share with your pastor and friends. Believe me, they will thank you for it.

Now it is time for you to carry the *fire!*

Brian Simmons
Passion & Fire Ministries
The Passion Translation Project

Introduction

FIRE IN THE STREETS!

Being born and raised in Connecticut, you cannot help but have a thirst for Awakening. Charles Finney, Jonathan Edwards and David Brainerd were all born here. D. L. Moody and countless others were born in these six states that make up New England. *Fire. Revival. Souls. Awakening.* All words that describe a period in America and the world that we call the Great Awakening. As a new believer in Jesus, I knew I was going to give my life to become part of seeing this again.

Little did I realize that within a month's span of each other, two events would take place that would completely change my life. My wife, Debbie, and I pastor a beautiful church in New London, Connecticut, called Engaging Heaven Church (EHC). And shortly after outgrowing more than one storefront, we were given an amazing opportunity to purchase a 750-seat sanctuary in downtown New London, a church building that was used during the Great Awakening. Many well-known early century revivalists like George Whitefield and Jonathan Edwards all had ministered there. This massive, gray-stoned, steepled church would now belong to us. I knew it was not about the building alone, but buying it would be a sign of hope that God was going to do this kind of awakening again across America and the world.

Shortly after we acquired this building, the Lord visited us in a unique way, and we would never be the same. We host monthly Firenights at our church, at which I speak or have different guests come in. We really set this time aside to contend for revival and go after God. One of my spiritual fathers, Dr. Brian Simmons, was scheduled to come speak on a Saturday night, but because of snow (of course), he was delayed and unable to make the service. I felt strongly that the Lord wanted us to continue whether or not he came, so I would just speak and we would do extended worship.

About thirty minutes into worship, I sensed something was different. The atmosphere was electric. *God wants to speak tonight*, I thought. During worship, I opened my eyes and saw a vision. Jesus was at the altar of this historic church, and in front of Him was a stone well such as you would draw water out of. On this stone well were written the words *FIRES OF AWAKENING*. Coming out of the well was fire—what looked to be liquid fire bubbling out of it.

Immediately, I felt God's presence and began to ask what Jesus was saying. I heard this: *I am about to ignite the Fires of Awakening again. This will be an end-time fire and will not be quenched. I am about to set America on fire. The nations will burn for Me again. This fire will burn in the streets! It will not go out! Burning ones will take this fire and reap the end-time harvest of souls.*

I began to burn with holy fire. I have been blessed to speak in some of the greatest revival churches all around the world. I have met some of the greatest generals of revival, and in my twenties I experienced revival firsthand. I am privileged to have relationships within many movements, and I have even authored a book on revival. I knew this was the real thing. Instantly, I realized how dry I was. In spite of my position and my desire for revival, I recognized my need for Him. I began weeping at the thought of genuine *fire* sweeping across America. I knew this night would be historic.

I went up to the platform and fell under God's power instantly. His glory was so strong. Before I even shared my encounter, people were weeping, wailing and travailing in God's presence. The thought of our guest speaker not coming was the last thing on our minds. God was here! After over an hour of worship, I gathered myself enough to share the encounter. Again, God's fire continued to fall. People were repenting of sin and confessing out loud the things in their lives that separated them from God.

There really was no sermon that night. God made it clear that He was about to relight the fires of awakening again. I was so undone after the service. I just walked into my office and began to worship at my desk. This was the very thing I lived and longed for. Nothing else mattered. Little did I know that the encounter was not over.

As I sat at my desk, I could hear people at the altar, still worshiping and weeping. This was well over an hour after the service. I still could feel the fire that was so strong in that place. As I sat and meditated on God's hand at work, I heard a loud explosion outside.

"What was *that?*" I yelled.

One of the ushers got up and looked out the window. "Doesn't look like anything, Pastor," he said. "Maybe a car accident or something."

It seemed all too loud and strange for it to be an accident. About twenty minutes went by, and then someone who had been outside knocked on the office door. It was a woman from the service, and she looked visibly shaken.

"Pastor—*fires in the streets!*" she exclaimed.

"I know!" I replied. "The Lord told me that tonight . . . so powerful."

"*No!*" she screamed. "Fire is burning in the streets . . . for *real*! God has confirmed His word to you, Pastor!"

I jumped up immediately and ran to the window. Sure enough, fire trucks were outside, surrounding the church. As I looked closer, I saw what looked like flames shooting out of the ground. I ran outside to see what had happened, and it was true. Full of curiosity, I asked the firemen who had arrived what was going on. Apparently, there was a transformer underground. (In fact, the word I had received from the Lord for the year was *transformation*.) This transformer had exploded and had blown off the manhole covers around the church. As a result, an electrical fire was causing flames to shoot out of every hole surrounding the building. Even after we left, this display of fire lasted far into the morning.

As I returned home, our house was full of bags packed for a trip to Florida. We would be doing ministry and going to a Disney resort where someone in the church had blessed us with a stay. Needless to say, our guest speaker made it in late, and he was scheduled to speak Sunday morning. Saturday night as I went to bed, I still could sense the presence of God so strongly. The thought of leaving for Florida was so far from my mind. I felt as though a day of visitation was at hand.

Fire. Transformers blown. It was all so sudden that I knew God was speaking. Manhole covers? How many Christians also live with "lids" that need to come off? There were so many symbols and messages happening. This was no accident. God was confirming His word with a sign and wonder.

As Debbie and I were driving to the airport Sunday morning, we decided about halfway through our ride from New London to JFK that we were going to stay and receive more fire. I knew God wanted to continue to speak to us. And honestly, after that service we were so undone. This was not hype. God was shaking us.

That morning, it did continue. Many people were touched, saved and healed. Ministry time lasted hours as Jesus began healing bodies and souls. His fire was showing genuine fruit, and many people began to burn again. I will never forget how after the service, a few of the "older" saints wanted to talk. I was not ready for the conversations that would follow.

"I'm sorry, Pastor," said one spiritual mom. "I realized when you shared the vision last night that I didn't really believe. I realized that I have been taking things for granted and have become stale."

This type of conversation happened over and over. I had to ask myself, *Could it be that in a Spirit-filled church where souls are saved and God moves weekly, people are cold in their hearts toward the movement of God? Is it possible that I have contributed to this stagnant lifestyle?*

I knew all of this was the result of God sending fresh fire. During the morning service, I called a special meeting for that night and asked people to bring those sick in their bodies. We would believe that God would burn up sickness, just as He was already burning up unhealthy lifestyles.

That night, with eight inches of snow falling, people came from all over for a touch from God. One man who had been hit by a car and thrown thirty feet was scheduled for surgery to have his legs amputated. He and his family drove many hours from Massachusetts to receive healing in God's presence. They had heard about the fire and the signs and wonders that took place. Our hearts rejoiced as Jesus healed this man. He ran up and down the aisles of the church, completely healed! His legs were restored.

Today, we live in an age where God's fire is not welcomed. Truth is, the word *Christian* used to mean a follower of Jesus who was filled with power and demonstration. Today, it is a term that does not demand respect. Many people have determined that the Church is the problem. We cannot continue to blame churches and leaders for our lack of devotion and surrender to Christ. Truth is, the people who do not like church (those believers who are in the "antichurch" movement) have actually contributed to the problem. We were never meant to live Christianity without God's fire.

The last words of Jesus to the Church are found in the book of Acts, chapter 1, verse 8: "But you shall receive power when the Holy Spirit has come upon you; and you shall be witnesses . . ." He told us that, as a result of His power, we would become witnesses. We cannot bear witness to something we have not experienced. It is possible that our knowledge can hinder us from the reality of knowing God.

The book of Luke tells us the story of the woman with the issue of blood. It is kind of crazy that her name is not mentioned and she is just reduced to an infirmity. Yet she was determined simply to touch Jesus:

> Now a woman, having a flow of blood for twelve years, who had spent all her livelihood on physicians and could not be healed by any, came from behind and touched the border of His garment. And immediately her flow of blood stopped.
>
> And Jesus said, "Who touched Me?"
>
> When all denied it, Peter and those with him said, "Master the multitudes throng and press You, and You say 'Who touched Me?'"
>
> But Jesus said, "Somebody touched Me, for I perceived power going out from Me."
>
> Luke 8:43–46

This lady had every excuse not to press in—infirmity, gender and theology. According to Jewish law and tradition, it was socially and theologically wrong for her to do so. The Law stated a woman with an issue like hers could not touch a priest. She was overcoming more than her blood.

Add to that the disciples, who many times, like us, did not realize or understand all that Jesus stood for. When Jesus asked who was touching Him, the disciples did not understand why He would ask such a thing; there were crowds of people touching Him, including them. When Jesus asked His question, I believe it was difficult for the disciples to realize it was about this woman. That very question of "Who touched Me?" was an indictment to His own. They were all walking with and brushing up against Jesus, and then this woman, who culturally and lawfully had no right to do so, touched a tassel! Not even touching Jesus, but something that was touching Him.

It is very important that in this day and age, we remember it is still about touching Jesus. We live in a social media age that has caused a generation to become numb toward relationships. We have thousands of followers and no friends. It has always been, and still is, about touching Jesus.

And many people who have walked with Jesus are hemorrhaging today. We have been in so many services, yet see very little fruit and results. We have watched thousands of hours of Christian TV, but very little changes. It is time to press through every obstacle and touch Jesus. It is time to break free from the fear of man and allow the life God created for you to come forth. You were made for history. Your life is not an accident; you have a destiny and a purpose, and it is time to touch Him.

We must develop a hunger for revival. It does not matter who is president, as long as we are living underneath where God has called us to live. A political party is not the answer. On-fire Christians are. Revival is the only hope for America. In this hour, the fire of Awakening is the only hope. It is seeing the Body of Christ mobilized for an end-time harvest. I have never witnessed more false doctrine and "anything goes" Christianity than we see today. I believe that one of the reasons God confirmed His word to us with actual fire in our streets is because He is about to separate His Word (Scripture) from every other word. God is a God of demonstration.

19

#Nofilter Jesus

Recently, I was preparing for a youth rally in our state. As I was speaking, the Lord spoke to me: *Who do you see Me as?*

I was caught off guard for sure. Of course I see Jesus as my Savior, Healer, Provider, Redeemer and Friend. So as I began to worship Him and honor Him with adoration and praise, He spoke again: *When you look at Me, I do not want any filter placed on Me. . . .*

Wow! I immediately realized that we must see Jesus for who He really is, not necessarily what someone else has told us He looks like.

We live in a day of pictures. Every day we see them. We take them. We use our imagination in response to them. Most people don't even take a photo today without some filter on it. Everyone is looking to enhance the original photo. It almost seems as if real-life color is not enough. Let me ask you a question: When you think of Jesus, whom do you see? I was curious, so I googled "Jesus Christ" online. I could not believe the image results from the search. Jesus looked sad in some images. In other images, He was holding a lamb or walking with lambs. In still others, He was touching His heart in a weird manner and holding up two fingers.

I have to be honest—I never pictured Jesus doing any of those things. And before you go throwing your grandmother's pictures off the wall or trashing your candles that have Jesus' picture on them, just wait. Stop and answer that question. When you think about Jesus Christ, what is it that you picture? Jesus may have been a lamb walker or a frail-looking dude, but that is not what I picture at all. Most images of Him seem weak, but I see Him as mighty and strong. Jesus was and is the most controversial figure ever to live. And how you view Him will determine the life you live.

Jesus said in John 10:10 (TPT), "I have come to give you everything in abundance, more than you expect—life in its fullness until you overflow!" Knowing this, it is tough to watch so many people not even live life, never mind more abundant life. We must be willing to look at Jesus without any filter. Jesus wants us to see Him for who He truly is.

Unknowingly, many people have placed filters on Jesus. Filters can come in many different forms and images. Maybe you have had a filter of false doctrine. Maybe you were told that miracles are no longer for today. Or you may have a filter of religion. Maybe God has moved in the past, and you have put in place an old filter of what revival will look like. Or you have bought into lies and allowed conviction to be mistaken for condemnation, and as a result you have lost your desire to live a holy life and draw near to God.

T. D. Jakes said one time, "The question is not *Are you blind?* but rather, *Where are you blind?*" We must ask God to expose those blind areas, those filtered areas, so we can allow Jesus to have free access to our hearts and minds. Revival is a way of life, not a series of meetings. It is the result of a heart burning for God. In Mark 6 we see a picture of some filters that got in the way:

> Then He went out from there and came to His own country, and His disciples followed Him. And when the Sabbath had come, He began to teach in the synagogue. And many hearing Him were astonished, saying, "Where did this Man get these things? And what wisdom is this which is given to Him, that such mighty works are performed by His hands!"
>
> Verses 1–2

Those present that day continued to doubt Him:

> "Is this not the carpenter, the Son of Mary, and brother of James, Joses, Judas, and Simon? And are not His sisters here with us?" So they were offended at Him.
>
> Verse 3

And the result of their offense and questions was clear:

> Now He could do no mighty work there, except that He laid His hands on a few sick people and healed them. And He marveled because of their unbelief. Then He went about the villages in a circuit, teaching.
>
> Verses 5–6

They looked at Jesus and questioned Him. They wondered who He really was. Were they right? Did they have the right view of Him? Actually, *yes*! He *was* the carpenter's son, and the brother of so many. Their problem was not what they saw, however. It was what they failed to see.

What You See Is What You Get

With Jesus, what you see is what you get. What you currently see when you think about Jesus can be a roadblock to what God is wanting you to see further about Him. What do you see when you look at Jesus? Is He just the Savior? That is all you will receive. Is He the lamb holder? Then all you will see is a pet owner. What filter have you placed on Him? Do you see Him as your Healer? Provider? Deliverer? Conqueror? How you perceive Him is how you will receive Him.

One time, Jesus asked the disciples an important question: "Who do men say that I am?" (Mark 8:27). That question still remains true today. It is so vital that you and I can answer that question. Many people see Jesus in a different way. We must see Him in the manner in which He came to us. Hebrews tells us that faith is activated by this principle: "But without faith it is impossible to please Him, for he who comes to God must believe that He is, and that He is a rewarder of those who diligently seek Him" (Hebrews 11:6).

Do you see it? We must have faith to please God; however, we must "believe that He is." This is so important to seeing

Jesus with no filter. When we approach God, we must *believe*. We are believers by nature. We must believe that He is . . .

. . . He is what? Whatever we need Him to be! If we need healing in our bodies, then we must believe that He is our Healer. If we need a financial miracle, then we must believe that He is Jehovah Jireh, our Provider. If we are looking to receive freedom from the chains of the past, then we must believe that He is our Deliverer.

I believe the fires of revival will unveil the true Jesus. He is the Way Maker. In Acts 2, Pentecost was about the Holy Spirit being given to the Church so that we can be empowered as witnesses. The early Church did not need social media and filtered photos. They encountered Jesus and shook this world upside down!

Revival on God's Terms

Years ago, Burger King had a motto: *Your way right away.* They wanted everyone to know that you can have it your way. Any burger, any item of food, prepared any way you wanted. No bun, no problem. Extra pickles, sure. Whatever you wanted. It was a ploy to empower the consumer with temporary power. We seem to love options, especially when we feel as though we are in control. We choose careers, clothes, food, cell phone providers and many other options in our lives. Somehow, choices give us the notion that we are in control.

Recently, we have been flooded in the Christian community with similar false doctrines. Contrary to popular belief, there is a standard of surrender. God is not allowing you to pick and choose a lifestyle to live. The early Church that experienced mighty moves of God understood this. Has Jesus paid for everything on the cross? Yes. Is it an invitation to live His life and give everything for that? Yes.

Revival is not "anything goes." It is not only the roof blowing off the place in a meeting; it is also actually the floor we stand on falling out from underneath us. It is surrender. America has wandered so far from her destiny that nothing short of a revival that sweeps this country is going to do. God has set out His desire, He has sent His Son to die and it is time for us to live again!

I believe that this is the greatest hour the Church has ever known. The greatest opportunities await. I believe the greatest worship songs have yet to be written. I also believe that there is a generation of revivalists of all ages who are being positioned to see Christ's fullness established in this earth. Heaven is waiting to be pulled upon to visit this land once again. This by far is not the fullness yet. Everything that you have known and read as revival up to this point has only been an appetizer for what is coming. Get ready for miracles in the wilderness!

At the same time, many are selling out to what they have always known. Many have accepted a cloudy word that they think is from God over a clear word. Many have followed people based on popularity and not presence. You may have left a church you thought dead in religion, only to embrace a prophetic version of the bondage you came from. Many have lost their ability to discern what is and is not God. Yet those who hunger for God will be filled. You were created to make a difference for God in this world. You are an overcomer, and God has placed you on this earth for a mighty purpose.

The Peril of Not Progressing

Hebrews 6:1–3 says that we cannot continue to lay a foundation:

> Therefore, leaving the discussion of the elementary principles of Christ, let us go on to perfection, not laying again the foundation of repentance from dead works and of faith toward God, of the doctrine of baptisms, of laying on of hands, of resurrection of the dead, and of eternal judgment. And this we will do if God permits.

There is the danger of continuing to hear and not respond. We cannot continue to neglect the things God has nudged us on. Obedience will change the atmosphere around you and cause all of heaven's increase to fall upon you. There is no such thing as having arrived in Christ. We are pursuing daily, putting ourselves under to do His will and learning to walk in the Spirit every day and in every circumstance and situation that may arise.

Not moving forward in the things of God is neglecting. Ignoring the Spirit's desire in our lives is neglecting. Not doing the will of the Father is also neglecting. It is important that you and I stay sensitive to the things the Holy Spirit asks us to do.

The Scripture is so true that says "we are receiving a kingdom which cannot be shaken" (Hebrews 12:28). We are continually receiving; it does not say "having received." It is not past tense. It is current now. Every day we are seeing the Kingdom expanding in our hearts and the reality of the supernatural forming within us. We have not obtained anything; we have been given the divine opportunity to receive the Kingdom and walk in the power of Jesus.

In Philippians 3, Paul also encourages us in this: "Not that I have already attained, or am already perfected; but I press on, that I may lay hold of that for which Christ Jesus has also laid hold of me" (verse 12). He continues to share what he feels is necessary for the Christian life: "Brethren, I do not count myself to have apprehended; but one thing I do, forgetting those things which are behind and reaching forward to those things which are ahead" (verse 13).

The beauty is that we have not obtained, but we press on toward those things that are ahead. We can operate in this abundant life now and yet press on to experience all God has for us. I know that hunger triggers heaven. We cannot act as if we have obtained. Thinking you have obtained is a lie to keep you underneath God's best. I desire more of Jesus because I know there *is* more. It is not a duty to love Jesus. Because He lives, we can overcome, and we can experience personal revival in every area of our lives.

Reaching for the Baton

One day when I was at the office, my assistant received a phone call from a reporter who was very curious about me. This reporter had heard stories and could not wrap her mind around why or how someone like me could ever be in ministry or even purchase our building. So she called and demanded that my assistant let her talk to me. It did not happen that day, but on another day when she called and I was in the office, I decided to take the call.

"Hello?" I said.

"Is this Pastor James Levesque?" the reporter asked.

"You got him," I replied with a smile.

"I need to ask you a few questions," she said.

It was not unusual for me to do interviews or talk to various newspapers and TV anchors about the different stuff God was doing, but this was different. This reporter told me she had looked into my past before calling. She had even talked to my elementary school teachers and old friends to track down as much information on me as possible.

"Umm, okay, if you're digging for dirt, I can fill you in on my life," I told her jokingly.

She said she just wanted to ask me the question that was baffling her the most: "Why *you*? How can someone from Branford Manor [low-income housing projects], a dropout from high school, who had no father and so many setbacks . . . how could God use *you*? It's as if God took the most unqualified person and decided to use him for pastoring a powerful church in the city! Please tell me how you can go from the housing projects, to leading a congregation, to purchasing one of the most prolific and iconic churches in all of America."

"Well," I said, "it really has nothing to do with me. All I can tell you is that Jesus Christ is real, and I've met Him!"

After I spent an hour sharing my testimony with her on the phone, she asked to come interview me with television cameras. I agreed. As I hung up, I was reminded what the Word of God says: "But God has chosen the foolish things of the world to put to shame the wise, and God has chosen the weak things of the world to put to shame the things which are mighty" (1 Corinthians 1:27).

God does not call the qualified; He qualifies the called. As you read this story, keep in mind that you are chosen for destiny, just as I am. There is nothing in your life that can take you out of line for His power to move in and through your life. You are more than a conqueror in Christ.

When this reporter came to the church, she arrived earlier than scheduled. I approached my office that day and realized there were cameras everywhere. Reporters filled the small office space. I sat down, and she asked me again to tell my story. As I began to share, I could feel God's presence beginning to fall in the room. The reporters were making comments about "such peace" and the "goose bumps" that were happening.

As I was wrapping up the interview, I had a vision. I looked behind me on my desk and began to see an arm reaching toward me with a baton. It looked like a regular baton, but the arm of the individual looked clothed in an older outfit, maybe early century. Getting this vision right then was all too weird, because I was in the process of filming and this was not in a church service or with people in my office who could understand it. Yet it was happening in that moment.

It's your turn to take the baton, the Lord said so clearly to me. *I am passing this baton to a generation that will believe me for revival and reformation again. Take it!* He exclaimed.

It was so powerful to me, though kind of awkward timing. Nonetheless, I stopped right in the middle of filming and shared the vision I was having. At that moment, I reached back and took the baton. I also told the reporters that the greatest revivals and awakenings have not taken place yet. It is only the beginning. This nation will burn for God again. From New York to California, God is about to invade! He is reigniting the fires of awakening again. This nation will be shaken one more time. History books will be written about these days.

The Kingdom of God is advancing, and the strong lay hold of it. The Kingdom is now, and we have only just begun this beautiful journey. What God is about to do will confound the wise, will cause fires to burn in the streets, will cause this unbelieving world to say, "Surely God is real and is in this place."

We are seeing it begin here, and I want to invite you on the journey. You were made for this. It is time to say good-bye to powerless Christianity and become a burning people for God. God's fire will burn in and through you in the days ahead. Get ready!

What are you waiting for? Reach back and take the baton.

Learning to Receive

For the majority of the last twenty years, I have been pastoring and planting churches in New England and abroad. I have the incredible privilege of traveling nationally and internationally, which brings me into contact with people from all different walks of life. I also have the incredible privilege of hosting a daily podcast, *Engaging Heaven Today*, which allows me both to ask and to answer all types of questions about what daily Christian living should look like.

What I am getting at is this: I spend a lot of time with people, particularly those who desire to follow Christ. And I love it! In nearly two decades of traveling, pastoring and day-to-day ministry life, however, I am continually shocked by one thing—people do not understand the fire of God.

You may be reading this and wondering to yourself, *What, exactly, is the fire of God? How do I receive it?*

Well, you are in the right place to find out. Recently someone asked me a question: "Why *fire*? With all the ministering you do, are you sure you want to be branded in that specific way?"

I honestly laughed out loud. When God's power touches you, you are not worried about your image or reputation. I want to please one person—Jesus! (My wife is a close second.)

Questions like these from people over the years have highlighted to me the lack of understanding about the fire of God. It is time we understand exactly what the fire of God is and how we can receive it in our lives and keep it burning.

The Bible tells us in Hebrews 12:29 that "our God is a consuming fire." At His core, God is a fire! On the Day of Pentecost, we saw "tongues of fire" appear on the head of every person present in that moment. It is interesting to note that the Father could have chosen anything as the symbol of Pentecost, but He chose fire. On that day, God painted a picture for us that the ignition of His fire is our source. For years, fire was the symbol of many Christian movements (the Methodists come to mind), and many of the hymns our fathers and mothers sang were written about it. Years ago, fire was understood and talked about. Today, we run from it. I believe that this lack of understanding of fire has contributed to the lukewarm Christian climate we are currently living in. If we do not want to be dying flames, we need to know more about the fire of God.

What Is the Fire of God?

Matthew 25:8 tells us that in the Parable of the Ten Virgins, "The foolish said to the wise, 'Give us some of your oil, for our lamps are going out.'" If there is one thing I have witnessed today, it is that many are content to live without fire and passion for God. When our passion and fire go out, we become dying flames—remnants of what used to be. Our countenance does not shine anymore, and there is nothing contagious about us.

It is easier today to compromise our message than to ask for fire. It is easier to change our doctrine than position ourselves for another Great Awakening. We are living in an era of skepticism and doubt. We need to get back to an understanding once again of what the fire of God is and what it does. Let's look at it more closely.

1. A Symbol of Christianity

My personal belief is that fire is a major symbol of Christianity. I would never presume to lessen the importance of the cross, but the cross in itself is easier to understand than fire. Malachi 3:2 says, "For He is like a refiner's fire." The fire of God refines us, burns sin out of our lives and causes us to receive a fresh baptism for God's purposes.

Part of understanding fire is redefining what being a Christian really is. The first mention of the word *Christian* in the Bible is in the book of Acts: "And when he [Barnabas] had found him [Saul], he brought him to Antioch. So it was that for a whole year they assembled with the church and taught a great many people. And the disciples were first called Christians in Antioch" (Acts 11:26). The early believers were described as Christians by outside observers. They were called Christians because they followed in the ways of Christ and studied His teachings. This name was truly the ultimate compliment. As people looked upon them, they could tell there was a difference about them.

Acts 4:13 (NIV) says, "When they saw the courage of Peter and John and realized that they were unschooled, ordinary men, they were astonished and they took note that these men had been with Jesus." What an amazing thing to have said about you. The early Church did not need Facebook, networking or Twitter. Their boldness *was* the advertising. People saw who they were not, but more importantly, they saw whom they had been with—*Jesus*. Are we willing to let the world see who we are not, so they can see whom we have been with?

2. An Endowment of Power

In Matthew 3:11 (NIV), John the Baptist says, "I baptize you with water for repentance. But after me comes one who is more powerful than I, whose sandals I am not worthy to carry. He will baptize you with the Holy Spirit and fire." Have you experienced the "and fire"? God has made it clear that there are three distinct baptisms, and we must receive a baptism of fire to fulfill what God has called us to.

Today the word *Pentecost* has lost its meaning. Years ago, if you identified yourself as Pentecostal, it meant you had been baptized with power, spoke in other tongues and believed in the full Gospel of power. Today, it either means you are cranky and mean, or it means you raise your hands during worship. Truthfully, it can be a joke.

God has designed us to walk in power. The disciples walked with Jesus for a few years, yet despite being with Jesus, they still lacked something. Jesus gave them a promise that they would be endued with power to be witnesses. I believe that this is a cornerstone of the Gospel. We must understand and embrace God's power and His design. He established His fire in us so that we could overcome. Speaking in other tongues is necessary, but it is not enough. We must be filled continually with the Holy Spirit.

Paul prays this way for all believers:

> . . . that He would grant you, according to the riches of His glory, to be strengthened with might through His Spirit in the inner man, that Christ may dwell in your hearts through faith; that you, being rooted and grounded in love, may be able to comprehend with all the saints what is the width and length and depth and height—to know the love of Christ which passes knowledge; that you may be filled with all the fullness of God.
>
> Ephesians 3:16–19

The word *fullness* here means "full measure." The word *be* means "continually being," painting a picture of being continually filled with the full measure of His Spirit. Somehow, all the Church has brought away from Acts chapter 2 is tongues. Friends, we have fallen so very short. The purpose of Pentecost is to enable the Holy Spirit to dwell within us, so we would embrace Christ's likeness and become like Him. His Spirit is made available to us so we would be filled with the fire of God, to be witnesses. Tongues is a gift of the Spirit, and it is very important. It was not, however, the point of Acts 2. The enemy has put a false finish line in front of the Church, and now we have tongue-talking, ineffective believers who do not win souls and have not been witnesses. That will change. Isaiah 4:4 talks about washing filth and purging bloodguilt "by the spirit of judgment and by the spirit of burning." I believe there is a new spirit of burning that is going to come upon the people of God for an end-time harvest of souls.

3. A Sign of God's Approval

In the Old Testament, God used fire to consume the sacrifices, and it was a sign of His approval. Leviticus 9:22–24 says,

> Then Aaron lifted his hand toward the people, blessed them, and came down from offering the sin offering, the burnt offering, and peace offerings. And Moses and Aaron went into the tabernacle of meeting, and came out and blessed the people. Then the glory of the LORD appeared to all the people, and fire came out from before the LORD and consumed the burnt offering and the fat on the altar. When all the people saw it, they shouted and fell on their faces.

In Genesis 15:17 (NIV), Abraham sacrificed five animals, laying them on the ground, and the Bible says "a smoking firepot with a blazing torch" walked among the sacrifices. Abraham understood this as God's way of saying *I approve*.

In Judges 13:20 (NIV), after Samson was born, his father offered God a sacrifice: "As the flame blazed up from the altar toward heaven, the angel of the LORD ascended in the flame. Seeing this, Manoah and his wife fell with their faces to the ground." Wow, the Lord moved, and an angel actually ascended in the flame!

That is what happens in our lives when we are filled with fire. Jesus ascends in us, transforming us into His image. Just as God consumed the sacrifices years ago, I believe that we will be the burning ones, a sacrifice God can consume in the days ahead.

4. A Sign of God's Presence

When God led the children of Israel out of Egypt, He chose to lead them by a pillar of fire. Exodus 13:20–22 (ESV) says,

> And they moved on from Succoth and encamped at Etham, on the edge of the wilderness. And the LORD went before them by day in a pillar of cloud to lead them along the way, and by night in a pillar of fire to give them light, that they might travel by day and by night. The pillar of cloud by day and the pillar of fire by night did not depart from before the people.

The Egyptians could not see it, but the people of Israel could. This fiery presence led them. God's presence was marked by fire. Charles Spurgeon reportedly once said, "A preacher must put the fire on a sermon or put the sermon in the fire!" Fire must be the fuel of our Christianity. Fire consumes us and leads us today.

We Must Keep It Burning

Proverbs 26:20 says, "Where there is no wood, the fire goes out." There is one condition on God's fire—we must keep it burning. God will send the fire, but we must be willing to keep it fueled and fresh. When you do not put wood on a fire, all you have is ashes. Ashes are a sign of where the fire used to be. America, along with many other nations, is primarily filled with ashes. Much of Christian TV—full of ashes. Many books, conferences, seminars—full of ashes. In many churches, passion and power have been replaced with potlucks and programs. When you are dealing with ashes, immorality is no longer convicting,

34

because we become desensitized to conviction. We live in a day where there is much debate on holiness and righteousness. It is time to receive a fresh spark of fire from heaven and reignite the fires in our hearts.

One of the sad examples of ashes left where the fire used to be is New England. I live in a land where God has visited many times and caused a Great Awakening to sweep through the land. When we look around today, however, there is very little sign of it. Many abandoned buildings, fields and barns stay empty despite being structured to handle what God was doing. When we purchased our historic building, the church that owned it before we did was not even meeting in the sanctuary. It was too expensive to heat, and frankly, they just did not need that much space for their small congregation.

When we purchased the building, we immediately "turned the oven on." We knew that we would build a fire again. And that is what we do as believers. We build a fire. We allow heaven to burn on our hearts, and as we prepare a place, God comes to consume. We have experienced a lot in the past few years in New England, in some ways on a historic level, but I do not believe we have even begun to see what God can do. We have only been gathering wood, preparing the brush, positioning things and walking in faith and power. As we feed the poor, win souls, plant churches and pray for the sick, we know God will ignite our sacrifice, and we will once again see another spiritual Great Awakening.

What if I told you that everything we have witnessed up until now has been looking through the keyhole of a door that is about to open?

Firefall

Yosemite National Park used to host an event called the Firefall. Each winter, Yosemite personnel collected hundreds of dead trees throughout the season and piled them high on a cliff. Once the day of the scheduled event arrived, a large crowd would gather in a safe place on a nearby mountain at nightfall. The large pile of dead trees would be doused in lighter fluid, immediately bursting into a great blaze. The crowd was then instructed to chant, "Let the fire fall!" Heavy machinery lurched forward, pushing the pile of flaming trees over the cliff, showers of fiery branches and crackling limbs cascading down through the night air. As you can imagine, this was a breathtaking experience, highly esteemed among tourists, a "fire spectacular."

There was a young man who, after hearing about the yearly fire phenomenon, was eager to see it. He saved his money and made the trip. When he arrived at Yosemite, however, he did not see any advertisements or information posted anywhere in the park. He asked a few fellow tourists if they knew where the Firefall was. No one he spoke to understood what he meant.

Growing frustrated, he went to the park office and asked an attendant, "When is the Firefall taking place?"

She replied, "We stopped doing that event last year, sir. The fire doesn't fall here anymore."

Because the overwhelming number of visitors that the Firefall attracted trampled the meadows, and because it was not a naturally occurring event, the National Park Service ordered Yosemite to stop hosting it. The Firefall ended in January 1968. Those who desire to know what it was like have to talk to someone who was fortunate enough to experience it firsthand.

In many ways, Christians in North America have been left with a similar experience. We have traded a convenient Christianity for "no more Firefall." We have built grand palaces and cathedrals. Week after week people come expecting a personal experience, and they are left with a show.

What we need is a Firefall. We cannot be content hearing stories of yesterday or simply reading the Word of God alone without applying it. We must experience the God of the Bible and allow our hearts to come alive again. Firefall is not convenient. It will cost us everything, but it will be worth it all. We will—we *must*—have Firefall again!

Convenient Christianity

We live in the most convenient day humanity has ever experienced. In many ways, it has made our daily life more enjoyable. News travels faster than it ever has, with the latest headlines only a tap, swipe or click away. As you are reading these words, if something urgent has happened in your town, anyone with a phone in his or her hand would know it before you did.

We buy our clothes and groceries online. We have food delivered to our door from any restaurant we want. Our television is commercial-free and on-demand. Everything from razors to music is at our fingertips through subscriptions. Technology allows people to connect all over the world, which keeps families in touch now more than ever.

One of the many challenges with all of the technology and conveniences in our world is that it has trained us to think that any difficulty or feeling of being uncomfortable means there must be something wrong. Inconvenience is a foreign concept in our society. I enjoy the conveniences technology affords in my life as much as the next person. But do you know what I don't want to come conveniently?

My faith.

Touched by a Hymnal

When we first purchased our sanctuary, it made major headlines. Many people wondered how one of the first thirty churches ever established in America was even made available for purchase at all, let alone for purchase by us. Truthfully, as beautiful as our building is, I have always been more passionate about seeing lives changed than about a building. It is, after all, people who make up the Body of Christ. Yes, the building is beautiful, both physically and symbolically. Upon entering those halls for the first time as the owner, however, I knew there were two things that would have to go—the pews and the hymnals.

Before you crucify me, let me explain. I did not grow up in church, and to this day I am unfamiliar with many hymns. In my thinking, the hymnals were a symbol of a staunch religious system I had spent my Christian life fighting against . . . until one day. One day when some staff members and interns were assigned the task of cleaning out the storage areas up in the steeple, I received a phone call from one of them.

"Pastor, I found some older hymnals. These are not the newer ones from the 1960s that we cleared out before. These are much older. Do you want to see them?"

My first reaction was to tell her no and move on with the day. But then I had a change of heart. These were a historical piece of our historical building, and I wanted to keep them. I asked her to bring one to me, and when I saw it, something caught in my spirit. I normally would not have given something like this much thought. But I sensed something more here. I did not feel as if this hymnal were old and irrelevant, which kind of surprised me.

I cracked open the cover and saw that it had been printed in the late 1800s. I began to think about the era of the First and Second Great Awakenings in America. I began to think about how D. L. Moody and many others broke spiritual ground in America and around the world at a time when the Gospel was advancing on the earth. They experienced a real outpouring of the Holy Spirit. I was sensing God's power as I held that hymnal in my own hands.

I opened it farther and began to read through the songs. Normally I would have dismissed them as wordy and difficult to understand, but this time I could not help but be captured by their content: *the blood, the cross, the Holy Spirit, souls, grace, power*! So many truths came to life. I knew as I read the lyrics of these songs that the authors had written them from real experiences. These songs were not born from pressure to write another song for an album or to come up with a Christian Top 100 hit. No, these songs seemed to be written in pain, in struggle and, ultimately, in victory.

I closed my eyes and asked the Lord to highlight one hymn to me. I decided that I would open the hymnal to a random page, and whatever page I opened it to, there would be a message God had for me. (Don't judge. You have probably tried the same kind of thing!) And there it was . . . on page 397 . . .

"I Need Thee Every Hour" by Annie Hawks

I need thee, O I need thee;
every hour I need thee;
O bless me now, my Savior,
I come to thee.[1]

Those lyrics washed over my soul, and I knew that this must be the cry for an outpouring of the Holy Spirit. There was something about this song that captured me. After a little research, I found out the story behind this powerful hymn. Annie Hawks herself wrote,

One day as a young wife and mother of 37 years of age, I was busy with my regular household tasks during a bright June morning [in 1872]. Suddenly, I became so filled with the sense of nearness to the Master that, wondering how one could live without Him, either in joy or pain, these words were ushered into my mind, the thought at once taking full possession of me—"I Need Thee Every Hour. . . ."[2]

This song would be picked up by D. L. Moody and sung at most of his conventions. This one young mother's cry would be sung and heard around the world.

Let the Fire Fall!

God is calling you out. If you have made it this far in the book, there is something more you are longing for, something supernatural. I believe God is about to ignite your faith and cause a fresh fire to come upon your heart. Your destiny is not finished, and all the dreams and plans within you are going to come forth, in Jesus' mighty name!

Wherever you are and whatever you are doing as you read this, *stop!* I want you to stop right where you are and lift your hands. Declare with me, "Let the fire fall!" Now! Don't whisper it—declare it. Speak it again: *"Let the fire fall!"*

Come on! Get ready for transformation to take place as we journey together in this book.

Living in Pursuit
of His Presence

There is no doubt that the current spiritual climate in America is geared toward unbelief. Blogs, video devotionals, sermons, books, *opinions*—these things are more accessible than ever before. Not all that is available for consumption is beneficial, however. In recent years there have been more people trained in universities than ever before, but the main focus is critical thinking, and faith is lacking. Education begins as a lesson on knowing what you believe and searching out truth, and then eventually it comes to the complete reign of universalism in the "educated mind."

Christianity alone is under fire in America. In the mind of believers and unbelievers alike, praying, believing, contending and fasting for breakthrough are no longer relevant. An absurd thought! We must constantly "hunger and thirst for righteousness" (Matthew 5:6). Our lack of hunger and lack of pursuit for a constant outpouring of the Spirit have resulted in the state we live in currently. We have to choose what we

41

want to be passionate about and pursue. Whether you like it or not, whatever you daily behold, you daily become. What you declare out of your mouth is exactly what you will walk into in the days ahead.

Declining Morality

A few years back, our state joined many others in this nation in passing a law that recognizes same-sex marriages as a legal union. Let me first be clear—that is not my personal view, nor do I believe it agrees with biblical truth. When this law was passed, however, it did not shake me, move me or shock me in any way. Christians in Connecticut as a whole, however—you would have thought heaven's army had been defeated that day! As believers, we should *never* be shocked when people who do not serve God or love Him do crazy things or live a certain way. Yes, my heart breaks for humanity, and I live and breathe to see souls saved. But I am not watching the world system's trends as my gauge for spiritual awakening on the earth. I am looking at *you and me*.

I have always felt that the increase of darkness on this earth has a lot to do with believers' current inability to believe and pray and contend. Light is only one thing: the absence of darkness. When light does not shine, darkness prevails. And when the light of this world—a born-again believer—does not speak up, pray or contend for another great outpouring, nothing will change. If darkness breeds darkness, then it will only produce more darkness.

We need to stop focusing on sin. We need to stop making the people of this world out to be our enemies. They are not. The real problem is unbelieving believers—followers of Christ who refuse to open their mouths and decree, pray and stand for truth. Yes, I believe the moral decline of a nation is connected to the lack of obedience in believers.

Trumping Faith

In the most recent American presidential election, I began to see a scary trend on the rise among believers. We began to turn our efforts and energy toward politics instead of toward Jesus. I absolutely believe we should be aware of our nation's elections, be vocal and active, vote and exercise our rights and freedoms. That is not what is happening, however. There is a ditch of politics and distractions the enemy is digging for any believer foolish enough to fall into it.

In Paul's second letter to the Corinthians, he says this: "And since we have the same spirit of faith, according to what is written, 'I believed and therefore I spoke,' we also believe and therefore speak" (2 Corinthians 4:13). As believers, we are called to speak up about our faith, about what we believe. When President Donald Trump was running for office and was elected, however, I was astonished at the number of people who suddenly became so vocal on political matters. Border issues, political parties, economy, health care and many other topics started becoming highly talked about among people who had just recently been silent. Facebook and many other online platforms became battlegrounds for assaults, ugly talk, arguments and all other such nonsense. What was most shocking was that these were people who claimed to be believers yet who never shared their faith, put a post up about the things of God or ever shared their personal testimonies face-to-face or online.

It is not right for us suddenly to become bold and vocal about politics or some outspoken president, but to remain completely silent on the one thing that really matters—another spiritual Great Awakening. And when the current political uproars begin to see a decline in popularity, it is only a matter of time before another uproar will rise up, and people will become angry and vocal again. And the type of believer who joins the fray is only contributing to the decline of the spiritual and moral compass of America.

If you are clear about your values, if you share your faith consistently and if you tangibly bring change to this earth, then great. Speak away! If your priorities are not in order, however, please consider taking that misguided passion and frustration out on the devil, and start contending to make a radical difference in America. We don't need worldly evangelists who take up the passion of the White House (or any other political building). We need Spirit-filled believers who rise up and speak.

Sometimes it is easier to give in to the herd mentality or to throw your opinion into the ring when it seems popular to do so. We have to stand for truth, even when it is unpopular. When our focus is clear, we will begin to thirst for spiritual things, and then our frustrations will be geared toward seeing another Great Awakening, no matter what it will take. We will contend for and pursue the things of God, even if we seem to be the only ones standing for those.

Heartbreak Hill

My wife's friend who lives in Hawaii has competed (more than once) in an ultramarathon called the HURT 100. This is one of the toughest running competitions in the world. Over a course of 100 miles, through the mountains just outside Honolulu, this marathon takes runners into thick, sweaty jungles where they must run to elevations of up to 24,500 feet. It is so physically demanding that out of hundreds who enter the race, only a handful can actually finish it. It is not for the weak or the unprepared.

My wife and I followed this friend's journey to and through this incredibly difficult race (more than once), and we found ourselves so amazed by the process of it, both physically and mentally. I am not a runner, but as a believer, running has always intrigued me. It is an analogy that Paul the apostle uses often in his letters to the churches of his time:

> Do you not know that those who run in a race all run, but one receives the prize? Run in such a way that you may obtain it. And everyone who competes for the prize is temperate in all things. Now they do it to obtain a perishable crown, but we for an imperishable crown. Therefore I run thus: not with uncertainty. Thus I fight: not as one who beats the air. But I discipline my body and bring it into subjection, lest, when I have preached to others, I myself should become disqualified.
>
> 1 Corinthians 9:24–27

Paul presents the Church in Corinth with this very vivid picture of competitive running. What many do not realize is that the apostle Paul was writing to a Greek body of believers. It was the culture of the time to be physically active, specifically in competitive sports. Paul chose a subject that people could understand and relate to. In verse 24, Paul says "but one receives the prize." He wrote this because in Greek competition, only the runner who came in first place was recognized. No second-place prize was given.

Paul also mentions being temperate and disciplining the body. When training for a marathon, discipline is required, and the Greeks were familiar with this concept. Training, preparation, proper health and nutrition, and exercise are the building blocks of success. Mental preparation begins way before the race. No true competitor approaches a race without first focusing on the prize.

But not all competitors are true competitors. One of the most prestigious and well-known marathons in the United States is the Boston Marathon. It is a 26.2-mile run that thousands attend every year. Among those participating, you will find those who are serious, committed runners, but you will also find casual "weekend warriors" and folks who have no business doing their town's local "Bubble RUN," let alone taking on the Boston Marathon. Recognizing this trend, the organizers of the Boston Marathon decided to lay out the race in a unique fashion. The first sixteen miles follow a slow, downhill slope. This allows everyone involved to enjoy the beginning of the race—the festivities, cheers, free water bottles, balloons and cameras.

Then it gets serious. Marathoners take a small turn onto a road carefully chosen by the organizers that is nicknamed "Heartbreak Hill." Those who design the track for the Boston Marathon understand something. Around mile marker 16, something begins to happen to the body. Muscles begin to melt down. The mind becomes foggy, and runner's fatigue sets in. You hit a wall. It is the point of the race when you face the weakest conditions your body can face. This is where the training and preparation truly begin to matter. This is where the race is won in the mind. Right when those competing begin to feel the fatigue and exhaustion, they hit Heartbreak Hill. And people begin to quit in droves. The weekend warriors are picked off. The kind of casual runners who should be at a Bubble RUN take a selfie and get an Uber. Only the true competitors remain.

There is a purpose to this design. The organizers wanted to weed out all those who were unprepared, in order to allow the real runners to finish the race. Those who are truly prepared know they must save their energy for Heartbreak Hill. They know that it is coming, and they have prepared for it.

For several years, the winners of the Boston Marathon were runners from Ethiopia. Ethiopians are known as some of the fastest competitive runners in the world. These winners were interviewed concerning their nation's ability to produce so many gifted runners. One of the winners replied like this: "We run uphill our whole lives. Americans run straight only. Our nation, our people, run uphill. We are ready for Heartbreak Hill. We know it's coming. We run to win."

The first sixteen miles are fun. You have crowds of people cheering you on. The final ten miles are lonely. No crowds. No cheering. As we read Corinthians, we are reminded that this life is a race. We are running for a crown that cannot and will not perish. We are running a heavenly race. So many who receive Christ as their Savior are like the early runners in the Boston Marathon. Yet eventually in this life with God, we face difficulty and trials—Heartbreak Hill. We are overcomers and must prepare, study, pray and mentally get the victory so we can demonstrate true freedom on this earth. Everyone has a Heartbreak Hill to climb at some point. And to truly contend for the fire of God, we must push through every obstacle. We must run the race to win.

God has called you to receive fresh fire and release it. Whatever hill or mountain is in front of you, let's believe it will be removed. In the process of praying and contending for the fire, believe that God will ignite a new passion in your heart. There is a prize on the other side!

Living by Design

"The steps of a good man are ordered by the LORD, and He delights in his way," Psalm 37:23 says. When you go to a restaurant or the mall or the grocery store, look around. Many people are like robots, walking blindly around with no purpose or anything in their life worth fighting for. Many people live today as if life happens by accident. They spend their time reacting, on the defensive rather than the offensive. They are the sum total of the barrenness they have created. Sadly, for many believers, their lives look mostly the same.

It is important to realize that our lives are not by accident. Every strand of the fabric of our lives is purposeful by design. We are people of faith (the just shall live by faith), and there are no accidents with Kingdom kids. Faith is a flammable material that God can ignite. We must lay down every distraction that is pulling us away from contending and being hungry for the fire. We must surrender to the fire, allowing it ultimately to consume us and bring new life to our faith.

Hebrews says this: "Now faith is the assurance (the confirmation, the title deed) of the things [we] hope for, being the proof of things [we] do not see and the conviction of their reality [faith perceiving as real fact what is not revealed to the senses]" (Hebrews 11:1 AMPC). Faith is *assurance*. Another word for assurance is *confidence*. Faith is the *confidence*—the confirmation, the title deed!

When my wife and I arrive at the airport with our family, we have gotten a confirmation number with our seat assignments before the day of travel arrives. I never wonder if there will be room for us when we get there. Somewhere on that plane, we have seats. Someone else might get the boot, but because of my confirmation number, I am assured with great confidence that there are seats for us. We have the proof that we have seats on the plane, even though we cannot see those seats yet. I have the evidence of a seat that exists just for me, assured even though I cannot see it. That is how faith works. We have complete confidence that it is the Father's will that we experience the fire of God. We have assurance that God is ready for us to live with an outpouring of His Spirit.

If you own a car, then you have a title deed for it. You do not need to show me your car to prove that you have one. If you show me the title deed, then that is evidence enough that somewhere, a car that belongs to you exists. This is true of the Word of God. And what believers need most is knowledge of the evidence of what they have. What most people call faith is not really faith. It is just highly placed expectations on incorrect information. When you know the Word of God, you have an entire book of title deeds at your disposal. The knowledge of His Word is our weapon for contending. This must be our strategy and confidence in pursuing after heaven for an outpouring. This is our weapon to help us run up Heartbreak Hill.

The devil may be trying to tell you that you are sick, that you will never have enough money or that you will never be fulfilled in your life, but he is wrong. Don't get upset! Get your Bible out, go to the concordance and find yourself a title deed. Look at your set of title deeds for a while and build confidence that somewhere, this book of God's Word you are reading contains a promise and a truth to combat every lie of the enemy. Everything you need is right there in the Word of God.

That is all we have to hold on to in this world. We cannot let go of His Word. It is our title deed, our confidence, our assurance. The devil will inject fear, lying about what you read, telling you it will never come to pass. What you need to do is say, *Talk to the hand, 'cause the ear ain't listening! I have the title deed! I have the confirmation number! The Word says, "By His stripes I am healed." It says, "My God shall supply all my needs according to His riches in glory." Devil, if I let you take this from me, then I don't have anything left. I don't have time to be bothered with what's going on around me. I don't have time to look around, because if I do, I might get distracted, and I might stop running the race set before me. I don't need an intrusion of the mind to cause confusion. I will keep speaking the Word. I know it exists somewhere (my breakthrough or healing or promise), and I don't know how long it's going to take to get to me, but I know it exists somewhere. I have the confirmation number and the title deed!*

We cannot afford to look at Heartbreak Hill. We have to keep our eyes on the only thing that promises us we are going to receive what we cannot see. "For we walk by faith, not by sight," says 2 Corinthians 5:7. That title deed in your Bible is still good, that confirmation number is still good and that assurance is still good. Don't you let *anyone* talk you out of it.

We are not moved by what we see. We are not moved by what we hear. We are not moved by what we feel. We are moved by God's Word. We are moved by faith and belief in His promises. That is the driving force that continues to push us to contend for fire, the real reason we conquer Heartbreak Hill.

Confidence in the Word

Faith is a practical expression of the confidence that you have in God and in His Word. When you sat down to read this book, you expressed your confidence in whatever seat, couch or chair you plopped yourself down on. You put confidence in its ability to support you. Without giving it a whole lot of thought, you sat down. That is how we have to become where the Word of God is concerned. We have to stop making it so complicated. We need to spend enough time with it so we can give a practical expression of our confidence.

Now you can see what the devil is really after: your confidence. That is why he works so hard to seduce you into sin. The blood of Jesus can forgive your sin, but sin makes cowards of men. Sin is what will bring the guilt and condemnation that attack your confidence. The enemy will work on you all week long about something you did a year ago, if you do not learn how to forgive yourself and learn how to have faith and confidence in what the blood of Jesus did. Sin, guilt and condemnation destroy confidence, and without confidence you cannot run this race. You cannot run after God and believe for fire if you are beaten down and pressed by the devil.

The greatest fear Satan can put upon God's people is the fear that what God has said will not come to pass. In order to give a practical expression of your confidence in God and in His Word, you cannot neglect the area of confidence and assurance. There has to be a little bit of cockiness in every Christian. You have to walk around knowing that you know.

"Therefore do not cast away your confidence, which has great reward" (Hebrews 10:35). The Bible is clear that if you lose your confidence, you lose your potential to receive a reward. If we run this race without confidence, we will not have an ability to finish the race. Confidence in God and in His Word is everything. It is what allows us to walk in confidence and power. Confident runners finish the race. They run up the hill and overcome every distraction from the enemy.

Confidence allows us to approach heaven with boldness. "Let us then approach God's throne of grace with confidence" (Hebrews 4:16 NIV). Our pursuit for outpouring is the practical expression of confidence in God and in His Word. If the enemy can get you to question what God has promised you, then your ability to pursue God's best is fractured.

In the Garden, God was pretty clear on His expectations of Adam and Eve. He said, "But you must not eat from the tree of the knowledge of good and evil, for when you eat from it you will certainly die" (Genesis 2:17 NIV). There is not a lot of room for error there, and most people would have stopped and decided to listen the second they heard the word *die*. The enemy knew how to work down Eve's confidence, however, by saying, "Did God actually say, 'You shall not eat of any tree in the garden'?" (Genesis 3:1 ESV).

It is not just the question that is the problem. It is the questioning of God's will and His Word that is the problem. When we hear a word from God, the enemy immediately confronts us, wanting to clarify and adjust the word that was just spoken. We cannot live confidently in Christ or come boldly before the Lord if there is a question about what we are supposed to be doing. Contending for God's power and fire will constantly require that you and I be focused, standing with Christ's confidence. And for us to see the fires of awakening and outpouring restored, we must continue to pursue Him. Get ready!

PRINCIPLE #3

Walking in Boldness

Boldness. It is one of those words we rarely understand but always want to experience. When Jesus came to this earth, He was sent to show us a better way. He was not sent to be God parading around in all His glory, but to show us what is possible for all men who have a new-birth experience. Jesus often said things like this: "All authority has been given to Me in heaven and on earth" (Matthew 28:18). I do not believe He was speaking as God alone. I believe He was explaining what would be possible if we surrender everything to Him and receive His perfect plan. Boldness and authority are some of the promises that are given to the children of God so they can carry out His purposes.

At the beginning of His ministry, Jesus prayed that God would send Him twelve people who would help Him turn this world upside down. (I believe He was very specific about the number twelve, which refers back to the twelve tribes of Israel.) The disciples came from all different backgrounds, from fishermen to tax collectors. And for three and a half years, Jesus poured His life into His friends. This band of brothers experienced power on never-seen-before levels. They saw dead men raised back to life, blind eyes opened and sinners delivered and forgiven and changed. They witnessed Jesus hailed and then nailed in the same moment. Even with those firsthand experiences, however, and with the teaching they heard and the ministry they personally received from Jesus, it was not enough. Jesus, knowing it would soon be time for Him to leave, came to them before it happened and said, "I am going to send you what my Father has promised; but stay in the city until you have been clothed with power from on high" (Luke 24:49 NIV).

Are you catching that? After everything they had experienced in those three and a half years, it would not be unreasonable to think that the disciples were ready to preach the Gospel throughout the world. But no! Essentially, Jesus tells them, "There is something more you need! For the purpose of your calling, you must be clothed with power from on high."

And none of them could have been prepared for what came next.

Power to Be a Witness

> And being assembled together with them, He commanded them not to depart from Jerusalem, but to wait for the Promise of the Father, "which," He said, "you have heard from Me; for John truly baptized with water, but you shall be baptized with the Holy Spirit not many days from now." Therefore, when they had come together, they asked Him, saying, "Lord, will You at this time restore the kingdom to Israel?" And He said to them, "It is not for you to know times or seasons which the Father has put in His own authority. But you shall receive power when the Holy Spirit has come upon you; and you shall be witnesses to Me in Jerusalem, and in all Judea and Samaria, and to the end of the earth."
>
> Acts 1:4–8

Jesus did not mention tongues. He did not mention fire. He only said, "You shall receive power when the Holy Spirit has come upon you." What does "receive power when the Holy Spirit has come upon you" look like? No one knew.

Can you imagine if we had been in the Upper Room, waiting for this promise? What do you think we would have been waiting for? If I had been standing next to you in the Upper Room, I would have elbowed you and asked, "Hey, what are we actually waiting up here for?"

And arms raised, you would probably have replied, "I actually have no idea. Jesus said something about *power to be a witness.*"

And that is really it. All that the people gathered that day in the Upper Room knew for sure was that Jesus had told them they needed to be clothed with power so they could be witnesses.

Before we take a closer look at the actual events of that moment, let's take a moment to remember that we were warned about this powerful moment before it ever took place. John the Baptist had come on the scene earlier with the same spirit and power that Elijah had. He was a radical prophet who was preparing the way of the Lord. During his baptizing ministry, John told us that Someone greater was coming:

> I indeed baptize you with water unto repentance, but He who is coming after me is mightier than I, whose sandals I am not worthy to carry. He will baptize you with the Holy Spirit and fire.
>
> Matthew 3:11

And fire. There was another baptism coming. There was Someone coming more powerful than John, who would not only baptize us in water or in the Spirit, but also in fire. The people did not understand fully what John was talking about. But they knew that something greater was coming. So as you can imagine, when Jesus showed up and also said there was something greater coming, it made sense to some of them. They had been warned.

Upper Room Confusion

I gave my life to the Lord at a traditional Pentecostal church. There were statements on paper of their belief in the gifts and power of God. The church hosted Holy Spirit Night services every Saturday night, which I was always really excited about, all geared toward people being "filled with the Spirit." We called it being "baptized in the Holy Ghost." Our understanding of it was that when you prayed and believed, God would fill you with the Holy Spirit, and the evidence of that would be speaking in other tongues—a traditional Pentecostal view. At these events, the people were mostly focused on the evidence of speaking in tongues alone. They would study and prepare, and they would tarry on those evenings just to get the gift of tongues.

Before I move forward, please let me explain that I tremendously value the gift of speaking in other tongues. I speak in tongues often, promote that others pursue the gift and even believe that it is one of the initial evidences of having a Spirit-filled life.

Paul said concerning tongues, "Though I speak with the tongues of men and of angels . . ." (1 Corinthians 13:1). *We must realize that the gift of speaking in tongues has a dual purpose.* It gives us "tongues of men," speaking of what we traditionally know as tongues and interpretation. I believe this happens mostly on an international scale with people who do not speak the same language. It also, of course, happens when there is not more than one language present. Secondly, the gift of speaking in tongues gives us a prayer language. When we do not have the words to pray, or we are confused about how to intercede, the Holy Spirit will give us a prayer language and speak the groaning of the heart.

With my stance on the gift and purpose of speaking in tongues explained, let me get to my point: We have foolishly made speaking in tongues the end game for living a Spirit-filled life. The thought that when we as believers get filled with the Holy Spirit and speak in other tongues, it immediately seals us and gives us everything we need for a Spirit-filled life, is silly at best. When we study the Day of Pentecost and remember what was promised by both John the Baptist and Jesus Himself, speaking in tongues is just a small part of a much bigger purpose. Jesus never said, "You shall receive the gift of speaking in tongues." He said, "You shall receive *power*." Could it be that most of us have been looking at tongues instead of the promised power?

I have witnessed so many people being "baptized in the Holy Spirit" with the evidence of speaking in tongues, yet who never share their faith. There are tongue-talking believers who never take authority or walk in power. This is not the kind of boldness the Bible describes. Speaking in tongues has become like a false finish line in the minds of Spirit-filled believers. The enemy loves that tongues has become the end-all of the infilling of the Spirit in the minds of believers, instead of the end-all being the power to be a witness. Let's remember that the promise the Lord gave us was that we would receive fresh power, and that when it came upon us, we would be witnesses.

Again, I believe in the gift of speaking in tongues, and I speak in tongues often. But I have come to realize that many believers have fallen short. They have allowed tongues to be the final chapter of the book, instead of the introduction.

Many years ago, a Gallup poll was conducted to see how many Christians around the world claimed to "speak in tongues." To the researchers' shock, many people claimed to have this experience. At the time, 500 million people on earth said that they had received the gift of speaking in tongues. That fact tells us everything we need to know. Two thousand years ago, 120 people were filled with the Spirit in the Upper Room and turned this world upside down. Today, well over that early poll number of 500 million claim to have had the same experience as the first

120, and the world has never been a darker place. Perhaps we must look again at the original promise and purpose. We must be baptized with a baptism of fire!

Power with a Purpose

When I was a new Christian, I can remember reading the Word and coming upon a passage that struck me and stayed with me: "Heal the sick, cleanse the lepers, raise the dead, cast out demons. Freely you have received, freely give" (Matthew 10:8).

As I was meditating on that thought, in awe of it, I heard the Lord speak to me: *Do you want a commissioning like that?*

I was stunned to hear it; maybe even a bit nervous at the thought. But immediately I yelled, "*Yes!* I want that commissioning!"

I was excited at the thought of Jesus giving me power from on high and sending me out to do His mighty work on this earth. After I responded, I found myself in a dreamy state, envisioning myself doing great things for the Lord. Then softly, I heard the Lord say to me, *Then find out why I commissioned them. Learn the reason.*

What could be the reason that Jesus commissioned these men and women? I decided to read Matthew 7, 8 and 9 to see if there were any clues concerning Jesus' commissioning of the disciples in this way. Then I saw it:

> Then Jesus went about all the cities and villages, teaching in their synagogues, preaching the gospel of the kingdom, and healing every sickness and every disease among the people. But when He saw the multitudes, He was moved with compassion for them, because they were weary and scattered, like sheep having no shepherd. Then He said to His disciples, "The harvest truly is plentiful, but the laborers are few."
>
> Matthew 9:35–37

57

There they were, the keys to being commissioned and walking in great power—compassion and purpose. Jesus was moved by compassion toward the multitudes and saw that they needed to be transformed, so He began to release those closest to Him with that same purpose—to touch the lives around them, as He did. The need was great. The crowds were lost, sheep without a Shepherd.

Imagine that Jesus walked up to you and, using the words of Matthew 10:8, commissioned you into the preaching of the Gospel. Powerful, right? Yes it is, because He *did* walk up to you and use these words to commission you.

What is the baptism of fire? It is simply a power from on high for service. If you and I are going to walk in power and authority from on high, then we must connect it to the purpose and plan of God. We must walk in the same compassion Jesus did and be moved to reach out to those in need. We must be revival and awakening on two feet.

Few Laborers

I have spent many hours praying for the lost—family, friends, co-workers, entertainers. I believe praying for those who do not know Christ is very important. The apostle Paul mentions it many times in his letters to the churches. There is, however, One more important than Paul whom we never see pray for the lost—Jesus. When Jesus prayed, He prayed for *laborers.*

The harvest has been and always will be plentiful. There are opportunities daily to reach hurting people. Not as common are willing vessels who will meet those hurting people where they are at. Most people live an entire lifetime and never share their faith, lay hands on the sick, never step out and believe that there is more power available to them.

Imagine with me for a moment that we are attending a church service together and two screens appear before us. On one screen are listed all the services and hours everyone in the service has clocked in their lifetime. Next to us is someone who has been in church services two times a week for forty years—over four thousand services in a lifetime. Many of us have attended even more services than that. On the second screen is listed the number of souls saved or people who have experienced miracles because of that same person. That number for most believers, sadly, would be fewer than five people.

The issue has never been the lost. Truly, the problem is unbelieving believers. It is time for us to take up the mandate of Jesus Christ, receive fresh power and believe that God will do miracles through our lives again. Fresh boldness is waiting for you. But it only comes through fire. On the Day of Pentecost, fire appeared on the heads of everyone present. They immediately knew it was power to be a witness, and they carried that flame everywhere they went. They carried the fire with no conferences or special speakers. From *fire*, they lit the world on fire.

In the book of Acts we see the proof:

> And he [Paul] went into the synagogue and spoke boldly for three months, reasoning and persuading concerning the things of the kingdom of God. But when some were hardened and did not believe, but spoke evil of the Way before the multitude, he departed from them and withdrew the disciples, reasoning daily in the school of Tyrannus. And this continued for two years, so that all who dwelt in Asia heard the word of the Lord Jesus, both Jews and Greeks.
>
> Acts 19:8–10

Even despite the fact that there were some who did not believe and who showed resistance, Paul and the other believers continued to speak the word with boldness. And they continued at such a rate that within two years, every single person in Asia had heard the word of the Lord. Boldness was the factor that changed the atmosphere.

Your Purpose

Another time years ago, when I was seeking the Lord and reading this same passage, the Lord asked me, *What one thing would you do in this earth for Me if you knew you wouldn't fail? If I gave you all the power, money and resources to accomplish anything, what would you do?*

I was shocked even to hear such a question. But my spirit was stirred, and I wanted to have an answer. Immediately following this question, the memory of a quote from C. T. Studd came to mind. He once wrote,

> Some want to live within the sound
> Of Church or Chapel bell,
> I want to run a Rescue Shop
> Within a yard of hell.[1]

The thought of being a yard away from hell—from the people you are called to reach, from lost people—has always impacted me. So when the Lord asked me this question, I sat for a moment, remembering what Studd had said, and then I responded the same way he did: *Lord, I would plant a church a yard away from hell!*

Now let me ask you the same question. With unlimited resources and God's guarantee that you would succeed, what would you do? The answer to that question is what will clarify your destiny. It is time to dream big and apprehend all that God has for you. Dreaming is the language of God, and we must truly begin to believe that anything is possible. God is the Way Maker. So many have stopped allowing themselves to dream. Without a dream, without purpose, there is no way to receive the boldness that God has for you. There is a realm of bold fire that is reserved for His purposes—on His terms.

When we are young, it is easy. We want to move away, sell out everything for God, take risks, walk by faith. When we get a little older, those choices do not seem as easy. When we are in our teens or twenties, there really is not a whole lot at risk when we make radical decisions. When we get into our thirties, forties, fifties, it is much more difficult. Radical choices affect family, career and the many distractions accumulated over the years. And often by the time we have reached our sixties and seventies, we have become a shell of all the dreams that could have been.

Many people do not experience the boldness we see in the Bible because they have no purpose or reason to use it. It is important to realize that we must be dreamers, running with God's dreams. When we say yes, we will tap into a realm of the Spirit that has been reserved for partnership with heaven on earth. *Lord Jesus, we say yes today!*

Last Words

One day while I was studying, I received a phone call from a friend. He excitedly told me that he was watching a documentary on Netflix, and he was clearly very intrigued and interested in it. So I bit and asked him what it was about. A few words into his pitch, he lost me. The documentary was about murderers on death row, and it was deeply investigating their final words on this earth. I allowed my friend to go on for a few more sentences, and then I politely interrupted him with my personal sentiment on the subject: "I don't care about anyone's last words, bro! Stop."

The call left me feeling a little weirded out, but it also triggered something in my thoughts. If I were actually to care about anyone's last words, whose would they be? Maybe a family member? Maybe someone from the American Great Awakenings? Maybe someone from the Bible?

Oh, wait! Jesus! (Duh.)

I would absolutely care about whatever Jesus said before He died. As you can imagine, I quickly opened the Bible to help me recall exactly what Jesus said before He left this earth. Please understand that nothing in the Bible is by accident, and if the Lord allowed something to be written, there was a very specific intention for those words. With that in mind, let's take a closer look at Jesus' last words.

How You Exit the Stage

Nobody remembers how you enter the stage of life. They only remember how you exit. Did you finish strong? Or did your story end in tragedy?

I think about Muhammad Ali. He was a world-renowned boxer, famous for his big ego and even bigger mouth. His trash talk was fine, though, because he could always back it up. Most of us, whether fans of boxing or not, have seen the famous photos of him standing proudly over his competitor, whom he knocked out cold. Unfortunately, that is not the final memory of Ali. For true boxing fans, the final memory is of him as the older Ali, getting beat up and having no strength. How you finish matters!

The Bible says in the book of Mark that Jesus gave one final speech before He left. Look at His final words:

> Go into all the world and preach the gospel to every creature. He who believes and is baptized will be saved; but he who does not believe will be condemned. And these signs will follow those who believe: In My name they will cast out demons; they will speak with new tongues; they will take up serpents; and if they drink anything deadly, it will by no means hurt them; they will lay hands on the sick, and they will recover.
>
> Mark 16:15–18

Jesus did not tell us to "go build big buildings and denominations." He told us to go preach the Gospel and heal the sick. He promised we would have protection as we go. How we have come to the place where we are in Christianity today is astonishing to me. What would your response be if I deleted your perception of Christianity so that, with no previous concepts of what being a believer looked like, you heard Jesus say this? How would you serve God differently?

The people who were there to witness Jesus' exit from the stage of life responded the only way anyone should respond: "And they went out and preached everywhere, the Lord working with them and confirming the word through the accompanying signs. Amen" (Mark 16:20).

Honestly, there is no other response. When the fires of awakening touch you again, I believe this also will be your response. I believe that today as you are reading this, God is going to extend the days of your life and allow you to see His power work through you. I speak to you now that your best days are ahead of you. You will finish strong and receive fresh boldness for the dreams inside you. I declare this with you in Jesus' mighty name, Amen!

Walking in
Supernatural Courage

There is a common misconception that courage and bold-ness are synonymous. In my experience, this has not been the case. I have found that when boldness comes upon me, it numbs me to fear. Boldness is a willingness to go, and fear is absent when that boldness is present. Courage is the opposite of this. One way to define courage is the ability to do something that frightens you. Many times when cour-age is present, you will still feel the fear. You just will not give in to it. Have you ever found yourself in a situation where you sensed fear, yet you were still able to face the situation in front of you? *That* is courage.

In this chapter, we are going to look at two inspiring bibli-cal examples of courage, and look at the steps it will take for us to walk in this great gift. As we study the lives of David and Jonathan, I believe you will receive a gift of supernatural courage from their example. One of the things God is going to do in this great outpouring of His fire is release a mantle of supernatural courage. You are going to do mighty exploits for

God! Supernatural courage is coming upon you for everything God has called you to do.

Take the Land

David is a central figure in the Bible. In the Old Testament alone, he is mentioned over six hundred times. Most recognize him as the shepherd boy who defeated the mighty giant Goliath (see 1 Samuel 17). This was a triumphant moment for both Israel and David. The nation watched and wondered what this unlikely hero would do next, but David's next move was one that no one could have predicted. He took the head of Goliath in his hands and marched the bloody skull eighteen miles from where he had defeated him. Once he had reached the walled outskirts of the Jebusites' city, he left the head of Goliath on display for the inhabitants to see. This city was Jerusalem, but at the time that David fought and defeated Goliath, and in the years to come, the Jebusites called the city Jebus and retained possession of it.

In 2 Samuel 5, just a little over twenty years later, David was ruling over Hebron, a city south of Jebus. Many years had passed since the death of Goliath, and as David ruled in Hebron, a dream stirred in his heart. He remembered that as a seventeen-year-old shepherd boy, he had defeated the giant and then had walked the giant's head to the fortress not so far from where he ruled now, almost as if to say, "I'll be back. And the God who delivered Goliath into my hands will give this city to me, as well."

What a bold statement from such a young boy! Courage always connects with dreams. When we receive the heart of God, we must always keep it tucked away in our hearts and not give up, but keep dreaming about our future with God.

With that distant memory, supernatural courage came upon David to accomplish one of the greatest feats of his lifetime—the return to the city of the Jebusites to reestablish it as Jerusalem, the city of God.

It is important to note that David was king over Hebron, which was a small city. He could have stayed comfortable and successful at that level. He had no worldly reason to take on the dangerous and life-threatening mission of defeating the Jebusites and occupying Jerusalem.

Courage will demand that you break free of your comfort. So many are addicted to safety, and that need for comfort repels faith. How many would-be millionaires, entrepreneurs, pastors, homemakers (and the list goes on) are missing out on what God has for them because they have become comfortable with their past successes? What you have accomplished previously can become a safety net that hinders you from what you need to accomplish in the days ahead.

David desired to agree with God to fulfill the dream God had given him of restoring Jerusalem, and courage came upon him as he went. And courage was *greatly* needed, because when David decided to take the land, his past immediately met him there.

Overcoming Your Past

You must overcome your past to be courageous. Three times in 2 Samuel 5:6, the Bible says David could not enter the city: "And the king and his men went to Jerusalem against the Jebusites, the inhabitants of the land, who spoke to David, saying, 'You shall not come in here; but the blind and the lame will repel you,' thinking, 'David cannot come in here.'"

Theologians and rabbis teach that the Jebusites would hang mannequins like puppets over the high walls of the city of Jebus as a constant mockery of the people of God. One mannequin was blind and the other lame—a picture of two of the three patriarchal heroes of Israel. Isaac was blind at the time of his death, and Jacob, after fighting with the angel, never walked properly again. Every time the Israelites looked upon those walls, they saw the puppets and were reminded of where they had come from.

Any time excitement dared grow in them about the promise of taking this land, the Israelites quickly retreated, knowing that two of their forefathers were being mocked. The legends of the Jebusites were so strong in the Israelites' minds that they believed these enemies were too powerful to overcome. It was psychological warfare, folklore passed down through the ages that struck these precious people down and defeated them in their minds. The Jebusites had convinced a nation that they were not strong enough to win. And ultimately, the Israelites believed the lie that "the blind and the lame will repel you."

Every one of us has a past. We have made mistakes. We have had times and seasons in our lives where we have not been the best witness for Christ. When we begin to dream and want to step out in courage, the enemy will hang those puppets in front of us, mocking us, reminding us of our past. Your failures are not final! The enemy can mock all he wants—Christ has given us the victory. It is not about us, but about the One who is *in* us. If you are going to be courageous, you must overcome the lies in your mind from the psychological warfare surrounding you.

It may seem that every time you step out, the enemy is waiting right there to remind you that you are not good enough. He lies to you that you will never accomplish anything. He may even try to distract you with your family and how you will be just like them. When you believe a lie, you empower the liar. The very word *Satan* means "accuser." And that is all he does—accuses you to the point that you think about backing down and giving in.

And then courage rises up, in God's authority and love, and faces the lies, exposing them. Courage gives you the heart to face a giant when no one else will. I am telling you that it does not matter if everyone else is shrinking back, scared of the puppets—*you* will be filled with supernatural courage, and *you* will fight on and finish everything God has called you to do.

You Are Not Your Worst Moment

Abraham was promised that he would have a son, though he was a much older man than most fathers. That was a lot for his wife, Sarah, to take in. The Bible says in Genesis 18:11–15,

> Now Abraham and Sarah were old, well advanced in age; and Sarah had passed the age of childbearing. Therefore Sarah laughed within herself, saying, "After I have grown old, shall I have pleasure, my lord being old also?"
> And the LORD said to Abraham, "Why did Sarah laugh, saying, 'Shall I surely bear a child, since I am old?' Is anything too hard for the LORD? At the appointed time I will return to you, according to the time of life, and Sarah shall have a son."
> But Sarah denied it, saying, "I did not laugh," for she was afraid.
> And He said, "No, but you did laugh!"

Sarah laughed at the promise. (Um, rude!) Sarah was so old and so hurt by the years of waiting for a child that the thought of a miracle caused her to mock instead of rejoice. Her response was so strong that God actually was upset by it, and they bickered back and forth about it.

Yet in Hebrews 11:11, it also says, "By faith Sarah herself also received strength to conceive seed, and she bore a child when she was past the age, because she judged Him faithful who had promised."

Wait, what? Sarah is mentioned in the famous Hebrews 11 "Hall of Faith"? Can this be real? In Genesis, we see Sarah scoffing at the Lord, laughing at His promise. And then in the book of Hebrews, she is being hailed as a mighty woman of faith. Which one was she, then?

She was *both*. And depending on when someone enters the story of your life, so are *you*. You may have had weak moments along the way. Maybe you have even laughed at God. But the story is not finished. You are a mighty man or woman of God. You are not a finished product yet. You are not your worst moment. Do not let the devil hang a puppet of the past over the walls of your life, when your story is not finished.

Courage Always Makes a Way

David was not intimidated by the mockery of the mannequins. He had a vision to establish Jerusalem as the city of God. He lifted his eyes to the high places and saw how God was going to make a way for them:

> Now David said on that day, "Whoever climbs up by way of the water shaft and defeats the Jebusites (the lame and the blind, who are hated by David's soul), he shall be chief and captain." Therefore they say, "The blind and the lame shall not come into the house."
> Then David dwelt in the stronghold, and called it the City of David. And David built all around from the Millo and inward. So David went on and became great, and the LORD God of hosts was with him.
>
> 2 Samuel 5:8–10

The wall of the Jebusites was broad and strong, but David saw the city's one weakness—a water shaft. A gutter. They climbed through it and took the land. Courage will *always* make a way.

We live in a day when people do not like being uncomfortable. Nobody wants to face any resistance in life. As soon as things become difficult, believers will say things like "the grace has lifted" or "my season is over." No, honey—it never began! Life begins at the place where others are backing out and turning back. We have to move forward from being a culture of excuses and back doors to a culture that runs toward and embraces difficulty. God thrives in the darkest areas so His light can shine the brightest.

When David's men climbed up that water shaft, it was messy and dirty. I am sure they got stains on their clothes. I am sure they were bruised and beaten up and smelled to high heaven. But when you are full of courage, you are willing to do what seems crazy to everyone else. Truthfully, if we are going to do all that God has for us, we must be willing to get dirty and even stained to the point of criticism. None of those things mattered to David. He had a promise propelling him forward and the courage to face the opposition.

It is interesting to note that Joab, who was one of David's famous mighty men, was one of the more "mature" men in the group and one of the first to climb the water shaft. When he reached the top, he lifted his hands and declared, "God has given us this city!" I believe that in this final hour we will see the older, more mature saints catch a fresh gift of courage and begin to face new mountains in their lives.

Thank God David did not settle in Hebron. Hebron was big enough for David's ability, but Jerusalem required God's ability—His supernatural courage—to conquer it. It is time we rise up and take the land of God's promise.

Jonathan and the Armorbearer

During the reign of King Saul, the Israelites were facing a hopeless battle against the Philistine army. They were sorely outnumbered, and not a single one believed they could defeat the Philistines. Except for Jonathan:

> Then Jonathan said to the young man who bore his armor, "Come, let us go over to the garrison of these uncircumcised;

it may be that the LORD will work for us. For nothing restrains the LORD from saving by many or by few."

1 Samuel 14:6

Jonathan was the son of King Saul, and he alone declared a mind-set of courage in this seemingly lost battle. He understood that it did not matter if the army he led was great in number or few in number. Courage looked at the small army he had and declared that God could defeat the Philistine army anyway.

Courage does not wait for perfect conditions. In the face of hopeless circumstances, true courage comes upon you and causes faith to be ignited. When Jonathan made this declaration, there was no natural evidence to back up the truth of it. But what is the *spiritual* reality? "So his armorbearer said to him, 'Do all that is in your heart. Go then; here I am with you, according to your heart'" (verse 7).

Courage will always attract courage. Not only did Jonathan believe this crazy idea, but his armorbearer also responded, "Let's go!" Then there were two men willing to be crazy together. Sounds like God to me. It is a snowball effect from there. That is how courage works.

King of the Hill

When you were young, you may have played a game called King of the Hill. The rules are simple—someone stands at the top of the hill (the king), and it is everyone else's job to remove the king from the top of the hill. And if your friends played like my friends, oftentimes this was accomplished by any means necessary. We played this game often in my neighborhood, and let me tell you, the only way to win was to be the king from the start. It is next to impossible to remove someone from anything when he or she is higher than you. It is an automatic advantage to have the high ground.

I could never tell you the dangers we may face on a true battlefield, but my little childhood experience with this game gave me enough knowledge to know that the battle tactic is true that anyone at the top of a hill already has a fighting advantage. Yet look at Jonathan's approach:

> Then Jonathan said, "Very well, let us cross over to these men, and we will show ourselves to them. If they say thus to us, 'Wait until we come to you,' then we will stand still in our place and not go up to them. But if they say thus, 'Come up to us,' then we will go up. For the LORD has delivered them into our hand, and this will be a sign to us."
>
> 1 Samuel 14:8–10

Jonathan's thought that he and his armorbearer would go up-hill and defeat their enemies was totally unrealistic. As the son of a king who was known as a great warrior with a mind for battle, he would have known that this was a *terrible* idea. Yet it was an idea clearly born of supernatural courage.

At this point, most of the Israelite army had retreated into caves for safety, convinced this battle was already lost. These men had their eyes on Jonathan, watching his next move. To them, it must have seemed as if their great leader and his armorbearer had completely lost their minds. Then the unthinkable happened:

> So both of them showed themselves to the garrison of the Philistines. And the Philistines said, "Look, the Hebrews are coming out of the holes where they have hidden." Then the men of the garrison called to Jonathan and his armorbearer, and said, "Come up to us, and we will show you something."
>
> Jonathan said to his armorbearer, "Come up after me, for the LORD has delivered them into the hand of Israel." And Jonathan climbed up on his hands and knees with his armorbearer after him; and they fell before Jonathan. And as he came after him, his armorbearer killed them. That first slaughter which

Jonathan and his armorbearer made was about twenty men within about half an acre of land.

1 Samuel 14:11–14

Courage That Causes Trembling

The plan worked! (What?!) Like David when he took the city of the Jebusites, Jonathan showed supernatural courage in the face of uncertainty and believed God would do something amazing. And He did. They took the land under impossible circumstances.

There is a land God is asking you to believe for. Maybe you need to believe for your spouse to be saved. Maybe your heart burns for America to be shaken with a mighty outpouring of the Holy Spirit. Whatever it is, we must believe for supernatural courage to see God bring an awakening to every place in the world and to our lives.

Jonathan and his armorbearer made a decision that shook the world—literally. "And there was trembling in the camp, in the field, and among all the people. The garrison and the raiders also trembled; and the earth quaked, so that it was a very great trembling" (1 Samuel 14:15). God literally moved heaven and earth for Jonathan. This shaking caught the attention of Saul and the others who were hiding in their caves, so they came out into the sunlight to behold the great miracle that had occurred, which led to a mighty victory for the Israelite army. This moment was a major turning point in the constant warring between the Israelites and Philistines. Courage created it.

Your Land

It is important to know that as we study these two examples of courageous men, God wants us to receive this same faith and courage. What is the land you are believing to take? Maybe you need to start dreaming again. Ask for courage! Maybe you need to believe that God is not through with you, and that He will use you again mightily. Ask for courage!

I had the privilege of speaking at a conference in South Carolina for those age fifty and over. Yes, you read that right. Everyone at the event was fifty years old or older. I spoke about dreaming again, and about receiving fresh faith and courage. It was an impartation service, so we prayed over every single person in the room for a gift of courage to come upon him or her. In my twenty years of ministry, I had never before witnessed what would happen in that room that night.

People in that room began to pick up their dreams again. There were more than a dozen people who had either closed down a church or had resigned from a pastorate, and that night they felt as though it was time to jump back in. They knew that they had received fresh faith and courage to fight again. One couple from San Antonio, Texas, had just stepped down from their church on the Sunday before this service. They now believed they had made the wrong decision and were ready to jump back in and take the land. It was truly remarkable. Missionaries, pastors, mothers, fathers—all stirred up and called once again to believe. Everyone united in the belief that fresh courage had come upon them, and that they were being empowered to stand strong and take the land.

So let me ask again, what do *you* need courage for? What dream in your heart has not yet happened? What lie have you believed? God has sent me here today to declare to you that you will live again. You will do everything that is in your heart to do. You will dream again and see mighty exploits in God. It is never too late to dream again.

Don't complicate this! It is about believing for God-sized dreams and then stepping out in the face of fears and daring to dream for the impossible. And just as the weary men of the Israelite army had hidden in caves, but then came out again when Jonathan defeated the Philistine army, I believe that because you will show great courage in the days ahead, it will cause many others to break out of their complacency, too.

Prayer for Courage

Father, I thank You for the gift of courage. In the mighty name of Jesus, I declare that today a new chapter begins. Lord, I speak faith and courage into the person reading this now, and I prophesy this over him or her: "You are entering a new season of courage and destiny. Even within the next thirty days, I believe you will begin to see a mighty turnaround in your life. As you step out, as you receive fresh courage, I see God going before you, opening doors that you thought would be impossible to open. Doors are opening as you walk—keep walking! I see doors opening that no man can shut, and I see God shutting doors that no man can open again. Courage! I declare it over you and in you. Courage in Jesus' name! Come on!"

Learning to Dream Again

I n the previous chapter, we talked about walking in supernatural courage. In both the biblical accounts we studied, supernatural courage was stirred up by dreaming with God. Dreaming is the language of heaven.

I remember that when I gave my heart to the Lord, I began to write in a journal about all of the things I wanted to believe God for in my lifetime. I spent hours praying and writing. I called it my "Dream Journal." I wanted to touch God's heart and keep His dreams in front of my eyes.

When your memories outlast your dreams, you have died. Many today are like the walking dead, living but not really alive, because they have stopped dreaming.

Give Your Heart a Reason

I heard Dr. Oz say once on his television program, "If you give your heart a reason to beat, it will!" I really believe that. I see this happen to people regularly: They work hard for years, faithful to a job, and then when they retire, their life is over.

They stop dreaming, stop traveling, stop making new friends. They stop *living*. They are dying, and fast.

I came across a study that was conducted over a span of about 25 years. The researchers polled and monitored hundreds of elderly people, with the purpose of discovering the main indicators that triggered a decline in health and even brought on death. To their surprise, things like excess weight, genetics or poor health habits were low on the list. The number one reason people grew ill and died was because of a lack of personal touch or engagement. When we stop loving and being loved, something inside us dies, and our physical body follows suit.

Living life—engaging in physical activity and socialization, having a purpose—has been proven to extend our lives. This natural physical principle is true spiritually as well. When you stop dreaming with God, when you stop giving your spirit a reason to soar, it won't.

Dreamers have shaped our world for centuries. As I was flying with my son recently, he looked out the window and asked me, "Dad, how does flying work?"

My response was honest: "I'm not sure, son, but I thank God for the Wright brothers!"

There is obviously a true, scientific, measurable explanation as to why a tin can with wings can stay in the air safely for hours and miles at a time. I have no idea how to explain the phenomenon of flight, but I thank God that there were men and women who went before us to create commodities and conveniences that give us a better life.

Steve Jobs had a dream to "put a computer in every home in America." And at the time he dreamed it, it sounded ridiculous. In the 1980s and most of the 1990s, only the most privileged families in the world were able to afford to have a computer in their home. When the Apple Lisa was released in 1983, it cost a whopping $9,995. (That would be over $24,000 today.) With that high-priced investment you received an unreliable floppy drive, only 1 single MB RAM, and a 12-inch monochrome display. And that was a highly privileged deal at the time. Yet not so long ago, in the year 2000, if you had $2,300 lying around, you could purchase a Dell computer with a whopping 128 MB RAM.

Today, only 35 years since the release of the Apple Lisa, there are over 2 billion PCs in the world. In America in particular, if you do not have a computer or a smart device of some kind, you are considered a minority. Research shows that 85 percent of Americans personally own a computer or smart device.

It is the dreamers of our world—those who see life differently—who fill the voids and move this world forward. It is the awakeners who will shape this world for God. The people God used during the Great Awakenings in North America were dreamers. They preached and plowed in New England and the East Coast of the United States, believing for another awakening and outpouring, and they saw it with their own eyes. America and all the nations of this earth are waiting for a new generation of dreamers to come forth.

The Dreamer Joseph

I believe there are prophetic road maps and insights hidden throughout the Bible. The book of Romans says this: "For whatever things were written before were written for our learning, that we through the patience and comfort of the Scriptures might have hope" (Romans 15:4).

The Spirit of God, through men who loved Him, gave the whole of the Bible to us for our learning and inspiration—including the Old Testament. We need to read the Old Testament with an open heart and understand that these books are a prophetic road map of revelation. If we study many of the central figures of the Old Testament more deeply, we will receive power and faith through their stories.

One of the greatest dreamers in the Bible was an Old Testament hero named Joseph. God called Joseph out and set him apart at a young age. When Joseph was in his teens, the Bible says that his father, Israel (also called Jacob), gave him a gift:

> Now Israel loved Joseph more than all his children, because he was the son of his old age. Also he made him a tunic of many colors. But when his brothers saw that their father loved him more than all his brothers, they hated him and could not speak peaceably to him.
>
> Genesis 37:3–4

Israel favored Joseph and gave him a special gift that set him apart. This coat of many colors was meant to stand out. It was meant to make a statement. There was no hiding this coat.

Meant to Stand Out

We live in a day where there are more followers than leaders. People will not think freely anymore for fear of being criticized. When people notice that I am discussing a current event or a hot topic on my daily podcast, *Engaging Heaven Today*, they tune in, even if they are not regular listeners. Why? Because they want to be told what to think.

People are afraid to be vocal against sin—to admit that homosexuality is wrong; to say drinking and drunkenness are sins; to call out fornication for what it is. The masses follow whatever seems relevant and acceptable at the time. Christians have slipped blindly into this dangerous approach to life where it is cool to doubt everything—as if lacking faith and always questioning God make you appealing. No! No, friend, it is not appealing. It is a spiritual death sentence.

You were not created to blend in. You were meant to stand out. When Christ died on the cross, a coat of many colors was given to you—favor, blessing and new-creation realities. Wear that coat proudly! Do not for a moment give in to the doubt of the day. Press in for a greater demonstration of Jesus in your life. The next time you are at the water cooler at work, be bold. When you are with your friends and feel as though you do not want to be honest, speak up. They see the coat anyway. It cannot be hidden.

When Joseph received that coat, he stood out. It no longer allowed him to be mediocre. He had to make a decision to be bold and receive it. With this newfound favor, however, opposition also came. His brothers hated him for the coat. And then Joseph started dreaming.

> Now Joseph had a dream, and he told it to his brothers; and they hated him even more. So he said to them, "Please hear this dream which I have dreamed: There we were, binding sheaves in the field. Then behold, my sheaf arose and also stood upright; and indeed your sheaves stood all around and bowed down to my sheaf."
>
> And his brothers said to him, "Shall you indeed reign over us? Or shall you indeed have dominion over us?" So they hated him even more for his dreams and for his words.
>
> Genesis 37:5–8

In Joseph's dream, he saw the harvest of the field bowing down in front of him—a sign of harvest authority. His brothers burned with anger over the audacity of this young boy dreaming in such a way. And then Joseph "dreamed still another dream" (verse 9), and the meaning was clear. One day, Joseph would rule over his brothers and over his mother and father (see verses 10–11). This sealed the hatred in the hearts of his brothers. Seemingly, it sealed Joseph's demise as well:

> Now when they saw him afar off, even before he came near them, they conspired against him to kill him. Then they said to one another, "Look, this dreamer is coming! Come therefore,

let us now kill him and cast him into some pit; and we shall
say, 'Some wild beast has devoured him.' We shall see what will
become of his dreams!"

Genesis 37:18–20

What was truly a gift in Joseph's life became an object of
ridicule from others. His brothers mocked him, saying, "Look,
this dreamer is coming!" I wish we all would step into a place
where we are known for our dreams! Can you imagine that?
They did not even call him by his name anymore. He was now
"the dreamer." And then they threw him into a pit. They tried to
kill him, saying, "We shall see what will become of his dreams!"

Dreams Make a Way

One of the central themes in the story of Joseph is this: No
matter what happens in this life, the dream prevails. When God
gives us a dream, we are usually nowhere near the full manifes-
tation of that dream. But through the pits of life, God's dream
will never leave us. As a matter of fact, it is what sustains us
through every trial. Your dream will make a way.

Today, I want to challenge you to trust the dream. When the
fire falls and we begin to experience an outpouring, dreams
will come forth. When those once-thought-dead dreams are
resurrected, know that they will make a way for you. What you
see in front of you at this very moment is not what you will
become. There is greatness in you!

Joseph's brothers thought they could thwart God's plans by
leaving Joseph to die in a pit in the wilderness. But remember,
the dream always prevails. Help soon arrived for Joseph, and
from an unlikely place:

So it came to pass, when Joseph had come to his brothers, that
they stripped Joseph of his tunic, the tunic of many colors that

81

was on him. Then they took him and cast him into a pit. And the pit was empty; there was no water in it.

And they sat down to eat a meal. Then they lifted their eyes and looked, and there was a company of Ishmaelites, coming from Gilead with their camels, bearing spices, balm, and myrrh, on their way to carry them down to Egypt. So Judah said to his brothers, "What profit is there if we kill our brother and conceal his blood? Come and let us sell him to the Ishmaelites, and let not our hand be upon him, for he is our brother and our flesh." And his brothers listened. Then Midianite traders passed by; so the brothers pulled Joseph up and lifted him out of the pit, and sold him to the Ishmaelites for twenty shekels of silver. And they took Joseph to Egypt.

Genesis 37:23–28

A brief history lesson—Ishmael was the illegitimate son of Abraham through Sarah's servant, Hagar. Joseph was the son of Israel (Jacob), who was the son of Isaac, Abraham's legitimate son and heir. The Ishmaelites were a source of pain for Isaac and his descendants for many years, a feud that was the product of doubt and disobedience. And then Ishmael's sons rescued Joseph from death. This is another reminder that no matter what you have been through, God can use those seasons of pain to become the most fruitful seasons you have ever experienced.

Dreams Must Be Tested

The Ishmaelites took Joseph to Egypt, where he was purchased as a slave for the house of Potiphar. Even when he was a slave, the dream he had in his heart continued to open up doors of opportunity for him. Almost immediately upon Joseph's arrival, Potiphar recognized the hand of the Lord on his life. Potiphar gave Joseph the keys to his home and made him the overseer of his entire estate. Joseph was welcomed into the house and positioned with favor. This was an unexpected and most welcome turnaround in his life. There was only one problem, however, and it was a big one:

> Now Joseph was handsome in form and appearance.
> And it came to pass after these things that his master's wife cast longing eyes on Joseph, and she said, "Lie with me."
> But he refused and said to his master's wife, "Look, my master does not know what is with me in the house, and he has committed all that he has to my hand. There is no one greater in this house than I, nor has he kept back anything from me but you, because you are his wife. How then can I do this great wickedness, and sin against God?"
>
> Genesis 39:6–9

Potiphar's wife proved to be an incredible issue in this miraculous position Joseph had received after almost certain death in the pit. And this was not a one-time proposition. This happened daily for many months, maybe years. And daily, Joseph resisted these temptations of lust and adultery.

This is an eye-opening reality that we must comprehend. If we are going to do all that God has called us to do, we must overcome the temptations and lusts of this life. The enemy knows the dreams in our hearts and will do anything he can to take us out. It is important to understand that the enemy cannot *take* anything from us. If we lose something, we have *given it up*. By saying yes to sin, we willfully destroy our callings and sabotage our destinies. In this world, the enemy only has three things to work with: "For all that is in the world—the lust of the flesh, the lust of the eyes, and the pride of life—is not of the Father but is of the world" (1 John 2:16).

I can assure you that in the pursuit of your dream, you will have to overcome all of these temptations—the lust of the flesh, the lust of the eyes and the pride of life. I have watched ministers, business owners, mothers and fathers fall victim to seduction and lies and give up on the dreams in their hearts. This went deeper than Potiphar's wife wanting to sleep with Joseph. The enemy wanted Joseph's dream. Likewise, you will need to make sure your heart is guarded, protected carefully from the lies of the enemy. Your dream will be tested, just as Joseph's dream was tested.

It Is Not as It Seems

Eventually, Potiphar's wife grew so angry with Joseph for refusing her that she accused him of attempting to rape her, although she knew it would mean his demise. Potiphar, who at first discerned the favor on Joseph's life, did not show the same discernment in realizing that his wife was lying to him. Joseph was taken to prison, falsely accused, with no one to defend him:

> But it happened about this time, when Joseph went into the house to do his work, and none of the men of the house was inside, that she caught him by his garment, saying, "Lie with me." But he left his garment in her hand, and fled and ran outside. And so it was, when she saw that he had left his garment in her hand and fled outside, that she called to the men of her house and spoke to them, saying, "See, he has brought in to us a Hebrew to mock us. He came in to me to lie with me, and I cried out with a loud voice. And it happened, when he heard that I lifted my voice and cried out, that he left his garment with me, and fled and went outside."
>
> So she kept his garment with her until his master came home. Then she spoke to him with words like these, saying, "The Hebrew servant whom you brought to us came in to me to mock me; so it happened, as I lifted my voice and cried out, that he left his garment with me and fled outside."
>
> So it was, when his master heard the words which his wife spoke to him, saying, "Your servant did to me after this manner," that his anger was aroused. Then Joseph's master took him and put him into the prison, a place where the king's prisoners were confined. And he was there in the prison.
>
> Genesis 39:11–20

It is important for us to understand that Joseph was an *innocent man* yet was still in prison. We have tolerated a Christian culture that kicks people when they are down, judging them by the season they are in. Listen carefully: You *can* be in a prison because of your dream. You will, at one time or another, find yourself momentarily "down and out" because of your dream. We cannot judge people based on their prisons; you and I do not know their story.

There were seasons of my own life when people believed I was done and even wrote me off completely. And yet, the dream within me would not die. When I was first saved, I cried out to God and knew without a doubt that He was going to do amazing things in my life. I worshiped daily, read the Word with passion and went out on the streets to minister and pray for people. But I was also very young, and I made some mistakes. I got married after discovering that I had a child on the way at the age of 16, and when I was 24, my whole life appeared to come crumbling down. My wife at the time became pregnant with another man's child and left. Seemingly overnight, I was divorced and completely alone. I had lost everything, and there was no earthly reason to believe anything would be right again. But the dream still lived on inside me.

Even in our mistakes, we must know that God is faithful to deliver us. The dream always prevails when we are surrendered to the Lord. Here I am over fifteen years later—married to the woman of my dreams, with three beautiful children, living out the vision that God planted in my heart so long ago. Undoubtedly, God is a God of redemption.

Never judge a person by the prison he or she lives in today. It is only temporary. You may be reading this and thinking about the mistakes you have made in your life. I am telling you that God is restoring and redeeming the dreams in your heart. He is the God of the breakthrough, and whatever you lost will be restored one hundredfold to you, in Jesus' name.

The Butler and the Baker

Joseph found himself in prison, totally innocent and totally stripped of the position he had been given in Potiphar's home. Yet even in prison, Joseph gained favor. He prospered in a prison cell. The Bible says that Joseph was given the highest position of authority over all the prisoners and their daily activities:

> But the LORD was with Joseph and showed him mercy, and He gave him favor in the sight of the keeper of the prison. And the keeper of the prison committed to Joseph's hand all the prisoners who were in the prison; whatever they did there, it was his doing. The keeper of the prison did not look into anything that was under Joseph's authority, because the LORD was with him; and whatever he did, the LORD made it prosper.
>
> Genesis 39:21–23

In this position of power, Joseph came across a butler and a baker who were also in the prison. One morning, he noticed that these two men looked unusually troubled, so he asked them about it. As it turned out, they were dreamers, too:

> Then the butler and the baker of the king of Egypt, who were confined in the prison, had a dream, both of them, each man's dream in one night and each man's dream with its own interpretation. And Joseph came in to them in the morning and looked at them, and saw that they were sad. So he asked Pharaoh's officers who were with him in the custody of his lord's house, saying, "Why do you look so sad today?"
>
> And they said to him, "We each have had a dream, and there is no interpreter of it."
>
> So Joseph said to them, "Do not interpretations belong to God? Tell them to me, please."
>
> Genesis 40:5–8

In the "setback" of a prison cell, Joseph encountered two men who had dreams in need of interpretation. It is important to know that if you want clarity about your dreams, *you must surround yourself with other dreamers.* These prisoners were blessed because they were able to connect with a like-minded dreamer—someone who would understand.

Joseph considered the men's dreams, and through the Spirit of the Lord he was able to give them the interpretations (see Genesis 40:9–23). The baker would lose not only his position, but also his life. The chief butler would be called up and restored to the right hand of the Pharaoh. Joseph encouraged the butler to remember him when he received his restoration. And it happened exactly as Joseph predicted it would. The baker was executed, and the chief butler found himself again in Pharaoh's house, at his right hand. But the butler forgot about his promise to remember Joseph.

A full two years later, however, Pharaoh also had a dream, and not a single one of the magicians or wise men in the employ of the king could interpret its meaning. It was not until the butler heard his master's dream that he remembered the dreamer in the prison cell, the one who had helped him so long ago. Finally, he mentioned Joseph to Pharaoh (see Genesis 41:1–13), and Joseph was brought before him:

> Then Pharaoh sent and called Joseph, and they brought him quickly out of the dungeon; and he shaved, changed his clothing, and came to Pharaoh. And Pharaoh said to Joseph, "I have had a dream, and there is no one who can interpret it. But I have heard it said of you that you can understand a dream, to interpret it."
>
> So Joseph answered Pharaoh, saying, "It is not in me; God will give Pharaoh an answer of peace."
>
> Genesis 41:14–16

Joseph let the Pharaoh know that the Lord was warning him through this dream that a great famine was coming to the entirety of the known world. He also let Pharaoh know what could be done about the situation and how to go about handling it (see Genesis 41:17–36). And in response, the king did something incredible:

> Then Pharaoh said to Joseph, "Inasmuch as God has shown you all this, there is no one as discerning and wise as you. You shall be over my house, and all my people shall be ruled according to your word; only in regard to the throne will I be greater than you." And Pharaoh said to Joseph, "See, I have set you over all the land of Egypt."
>
> Genesis 41:39–41

Joseph went from the bowels of a prison cell to the second-most-powerful man in the world in just one moment. Suddenly, Joseph's own dream from all those years ago was realized, and the pain from the decades of trials he had faced alone was validated. *That* is the power of a dream. *That* is the God we serve.

I believe that when the fire falls, you are going to dream new dreams. I also believe that the dead dreams inside you will be resurrected.

Joseph's life is a prophetic picture of an overcoming generation that will soon arise on the earth. The dream in you will not die. God is working all of it out even now, right relationships and connections all coming into perfect alignment. Radical dreamers will be the mark of an outpouring of fire in this next generation.

Go for it, Joseph of today. The world is waiting for what God is going to do with *you*. You are a dreamer—so *dream*. I declare in the mighty name of Jesus, *dreamers, come forth!*

Living with
Holy Spirit Increase

I was in a meeting in British Columbia many years ago, and the minister said toward the end of the service, "Tomorrow night, I believe God will supernaturally cancel debt!" He urged everyone to come the next night with a symbol of his or her debt to lay on the altar.

In all honesty, I struggled with the idea at first. I realized that people's debt was just that—*their own debt*. If people fall into the bondage of debt with the full knowledge of what it is, why would God supernaturally set them free? I knew this minister as a friend, but that did not make the idea of God canceling debt less weird for me.

We attended the meeting the following night, and my wife (whom I was dating at the time) brought a tassel from her university. She believed that God was supernaturally going to cancel the student loan she had. Likewise, many people that night—hundreds!—brought medical bills, car payment bills, mortgages and many other items that represented a debt they owed. It was so difficult to comprehend for me, but I also knew that God is powerful enough to do it. I knew that He could do anything at any time.

As the worship began, the Lord began to deal with me, telling me, *I want you to know My principles about giving and receiving.* He went on to say, *Once you understand these principles, teach My Word in the area of giving.* I was undone. Not yet knowing what I would witness that night, I prepared my heart to receive this understanding of His Word concerning giving and being blessed. And within a year, Debbie and I saw $75,000 of our combined debt paid off, without any extra income on our part!

I believe debt is a curse. It is lack and is not God's best for us. We live in a day, however, when sometimes you cannot escape it. I believe God wants us to be debt free. While that means responsibly paying on the debts that we owe, even more important is the principle of believing for debt cancelation. Many people feel as though it is their debt, so it is their mistake or their fault. The thought that God can and will do things so outside of our understanding in regard to our debt is what is amazing, and it draws us into knowing more about His nature.

Letting Go of the Abuse

Anytime I teach about giving, people get weird. I get it. You probably were abused by some busted 1980s televangelist, and you are still angry about it. Or more likely, some pastor you knew (or maybe did not even know) took the church's tithes and moved to Hawaii. Or maybe he sold the church building and lived off the money. Regardless of the situation, any and all of those things are sinful (lying *and* stealing!), and those people will answer to God.

But what about you? Your personal response to giving and receiving will always expose your heart. Jesus said this: "No servant can serve two masters; for either he will hate the one and love the other, or else he will be loyal to the one and despise the other. You cannot serve God and mammon" (Luke 16:13).

This sums it up perfectly—you cannot serve God and money. You will love one and despise the other. Most people love money and despise the message of giving, which is the heart of the message of the Kingdom. Understanding the blessing of the Lord has very little to do with money; it has everything to do with understanding the God you serve. Look at the cross. With a single event, Christ defeated death, hell and the grave—in one moment! He paid the ultimate price so we would live blessed.

I have been pastoring for over twenty years. I have traveled over a million miles around the globe. In each of those twenty years and along each of those million miles, I have discovered that most believers have no clue how good God is. Our church feeds thousands of people a month locally, giving to families in need in our community. But lacking money is not the problem in these people's lives. Their understanding of God is.

God Is the Source

It is likely that you have a job, or have had one at some point in your life. It is also likely that you have received some sort of training for that job. You may have even attended a university to get a degree. All of this was done for the purpose of earning money so you could live your life. People go to great lengths to obtain money, yet rarely do they consider that it is God who gives us the power to create wealth: "And you shall remember the LORD your God, for it is He who gives you power to get wealth, that He may establish His covenant which He swore to your fathers, as it is this day" (Deuteronomy 8:18).

God is your source. Not a job. Not a spouse. Not a church. Nothing else but God. When I received this understanding, it began to transform my life. I never again looked to the methods of men to provide for me. If He chooses to use people, then wonderful! But they are *not* my source. I am a pastor, but let me tell you—the church I serve is not the source. God is! He has and always will continue to provide. It is about trust. We have to trust that it is only God who brings us promotion.

Psalm 75 says this: "For exaltation comes neither from the east nor from the west nor from the south. But God is the Judge: He puts down one, and exalts another" (verses 6–7).

God is the one who brings promotion. If our eyes are on anything other than Him, we will get sidetracked in life. We cannot be so busy making a living that we fail to make a life. He has given us a prescription in His Word for right living, and for living a life of generosity. The problem with the rat race is that at the end of the day, *you are still a rat.*

Everything We Will Ever Need

Everything we will ever need is available to us as believers. We do not have to work to get it. It is already on the inside of us. Incorrect teaching and wrong thoughts have made it very challenging for believers to access this great wealth inside them. It is like dying of thirst in the desert when you are leaning on the side of a well. We need to put our well-leaning days to an end and lower our buckets into the water that has been made available through Christ Jesus.

God wants to give us increase, but we have to give Him something to work with. We have opportunities every day—church, missions, blessing those in need. There is never a lack of opportunity to give and then trust God.

A few years ago, I noticed that churchgoers tend to get spiritually lazy in the summer. They just coast through the season, waiting for fall to arrive before they commit again. In response to this, our church held a series of meetings every weekend of the summer called "The Summer of Fire." We were basically saying this: "Give God your summer and see what He will do with it!" And He definitely blessed the efforts of those who gave Him their summer.

God's language is multiplication. Whatever we entrust to Him, He only knows how to bless it. We see these truths highlighted in the Matthew 14 story of the feeding of the five thousand:

> As evening approached, the disciples came to him and said, "This is a remote place, and it's already getting late. Send the crowds away, so they can go to the villages and buy themselves some food."
>
> Jesus replied, "They do not need to go away. You give them something to eat."
>
> "We have here only five loaves of bread and two fish," they answered.
>
> "Bring them here to me," he said. And he directed the people to sit down on the grass. Taking the five loaves and the two fish and looking up to heaven, he gave thanks and broke the loaves. Then he gave them to the disciples, and the disciples gave them to the people. They all ate and were satisfied, and the disciples picked up twelve basketfuls of broken pieces that were left over.
>
> Verses 15–20 NIV

There are a few things we need to note from this story. This miracle of multiplication required *faith*. It required that the disciples give Jesus somewhere to start. Even though what they offered was nowhere near enough under natural circumstances, they gave it to Jesus anyway. And as the gospel of John tells us, the starting point was a child's lunch—meaning the child gave something in faith first (see John 6:9).

To the carnal mind, it is preposterous to accept that in a situation of great need, a child offered up an answer. Know and understand this: God loves to receive from us the little things. The things that we have put on the back shelf, that we feel are insignificant, even the little foxes that seem persistent in our

93

lives (see Song of Solomon 2:15) . . . God wants them. God loves to work miracles through our lives, but it is our giving to Him that is the fuel for His vehicle of provision.

Do Not Confuse Your Confession

You will notice when you read the account of the loaves and fish that Jesus never confused His confession. He knew in the natural that five loaves of bread and two fish were not enough to feed thousands of people. And never once did Jesus speak of the lack in front of Him. We must take our eyes off the areas of lack in our lives. We have within us access to everything we will ever need through Jesus. Yet how many times do you hear believers confusing their confession? They will say,

"I can't afford that!"
"My kids don't listen!"
"I wish I had a nice house."
"I wish a man would love me."
"I never get nice things!"
"I'll never be able to go on a holiday."
"I'm broke!"

And so on, and so on. You will receive (or not receive) exactly what you believe.

There was *clearly* a situation of lack in Matthew 14. Yet at go time, you do not once see Jesus focus on what He does not have. I have seen people lose their minds at a small dinner party because the punch was running out. Here you have thousands ready to eat, with basically no food and no money to purchase any provisions, and Jesus never even flinches.

Too often we plan in the natural, put our trust in our paychecks or put our confidence in another person. But God is calling us to see things differently. Let's step out from the crowd and see the abundance. Sadly, so many will never see abundance in their lives because they do not understand their Source.

Too many believers are having sleepless nights because they do not realize that they have peace living inside them. Too many live with wayward children because they do not understand that it is their duty to train those children in the way that they should go. Too many live in poverty because they are unwilling to open their hands, not realizing that it is in giving that multiplication occurs. Do not confuse your confession!

Once the disciples gave Jesus the fish and the loaves, He blessed the food, commanded the supernatural power of God, performed the miracle and then gave the food back to the disciples to give to the people. It was in the giving out that multiplication happened. So often, we are in the middle of a miracle from God and we stop short because we are not sure the supply will continue. So we "get ours," but we never have enough to share with others. We need that continued supply to teach our families, to leave to our children, to trust again. It is almost as if we have a checklist of godly things we need to experience, and we check off *God provided*. But in our heart of hearts, we know that we stopped short. We punched out on our "believing time card," only for it to be stored on the shelf, brought out occasionally to impress others.

It reminds me of when people go on a fast and see breakthrough in an area. They did not realize that breakthrough was already theirs before they did something to try to earn it. Fasting, like giving, is for us, not for God. It is for the purpose of getting our minds right, refocused and set on Him. It is to prove to ourselves that we trust Him, not to get God to do something. He has *already done* everything He is ever going to do. Now it is time for us to obey Him.

Do not be that horribly dehydrated person who is leaning on a well in the desert. You already have everything you need.

There is always more with God—more healing, more joy, more peace, more resources, more relationships and more life. Do not look at your lack today in whatever area and use it as a mental stop sign. Give those areas of lack to God and watch the multiplication begin.

When Debbie and I found out we were pregnant, we wanted to buy some things in preparation for the baby. We did not have thousands of dollars sitting in a separate account labeled "Everything the Baby Needs and Wants." But we do have a well, and we know how to access the water. We are good stewards of the resources God has given us. We have been given much, and so, much is also required of us (see Luke 12:48). We trust and look to the Source, and every step of the way, God provides.

So when we were preparing for the baby, we were not going to settle for less on some bigger-ticket items we wanted. We believed God. We sowed for months. Let me tell you, God provided miraculously every single time! And if we received a gift, we gave an offering because of it. If we received a $25 gift card, then $2.50 went back into the offering. We did not stop along the way to consider what was not happening. We always thanked God and continued to give. We knew that if we had extra money that week and it was not enough to meet the need of one of those items, then it was to be considered seed, meaning we sowed it. It is all about trust—trusting that God will provide for me what I need, according to His riches and glory (which is better than ours). "And my God shall supply all your need according to His riches in glory by Christ Jesus" (Philippians 4:19).

During that season of sowing and believing, we returned home from a ministry trip to Florida and found a shocking surprise. Actually, many shocking surprises. About one hundred boxes were waiting for us on our front porch. They were gifts for our new baby, and they were exactly what we needed and had believed God for. We did not pay a single cent for those gifts, but we absolutely gave for them. On top of what God was already doing in other areas of our lives, He also provided for our baby because we gave what was in our hands. (And we knew that the multiplication would continue. The people who had put the gifts on our porch in the first place would also be blessed because they had given to us what was in their hands.)

Do not stop giving. When you stop giving, the multiplication miracle stops as well.

When Jesus finished feeding the multitudes, not only had people been fed until they were satisfied, but there were leftovers. God wants to use whatever you have in your hand to prove Himself mighty on your behalf. God has done all He is ever going to do. Now it is time for you to stop dying of thirst, just leaning on the well. It is time to access that water. God wants to give you increase. He wants to give you the desires of your heart. He wants to take the barren areas of your life and turn them into a land of plenty. But He needs you to give them to Him first.

God will turn your little into much. He will be able to get you a raise, even if He needs to give everyone else in the company a raise in order to get you what you need. He will be able to get you the peace in your heart you need, so you are not terrorized by your thought life. He will take your barren womb and give you children. He will change the heart of your spouse through His goodness on your life. He will bless your money so you can bless others. He will take your mouth and use your words for increase instead of doubt. You will look different. You will look like *Him*. But first, you have to understand His principles on giving and receiving.

What Are You Settling For?

When the fire of God falls, the blessing of the Lord will fall also. You will have to make a decision—how much do you want? An outpouring of the Holy Spirit is an invitation for more. When the Holy Spirit is poured out, we immediately realize our lack.

When my wife and I were first married, we were seeing God move so powerfully as we were traveling all over the world and speaking nightly. One night after a powerful meeting in Saint John, New Brunswick, as we were lying down to sleep, I heard the Lord say, *I want more of you.*

I was floored. I had no idea how I could physically do more for God. But God was not asking for me to *do* more—He was asking for me to *give more of me.* He wanted every area of my life, and if I would give Him my all, as a result it would increase my capacity to receive.

I am not just talking about finances. Honestly, finances are a very small part of living blessed and in abundance. It just happens to be an area where many people suffer. Let me be clear—the blessing of the Lord will overtake *every area of your life.* Peace, power, freedom, healing and life will overtake you when the blessing of the Lord does.

Charles Finney defined *revival* as a renewed obedience to God. I understand why he believed that to be true. We are not experiencing or chasing anything outside the Word of God or what God has already ordained. We are simply receiving more of it and all of it!

A Well of Blessing

We must decide whether we want a *cup* of blessing or a *well* of blessing. "What shall I render to the LORD for all His benefits toward me? I will take up the cup of salvation, and call upon the name of the LORD" (Psalm 116:12–13). In the Old Testament, salvation was mostly described as being a cup. David famously said "my cup runneth over" in Psalm 23 (KJV).

God chose to use a cup as an illustration for the measure of salvation and blessings before Christ. That changed, however, when Jesus arrived. Now our *cup* of salvation has been transformed into a *well*. The story of the woman at the well in John 4 is a great example of this truth. This woman went to a well, and then she *became* a well.

When Jesus encountered this Samaritan woman at the well, it is most likely that she was a prostitute, someone who had a shameful past and was looked down on by society. Yet He approached her to ask for a drink: "A woman of Samaria came to draw water. Jesus said to her, 'Give Me a drink.' For His disciples had gone away into the city to buy food" (John 4:7–8).

Jesus was not thirsty, but was actually asking her what she was thirsty for. She immediately replied that He had nothing to draw water with. This is the problem with a "cup mentality." Someone with a cup mentality never has enough and is never equipped properly. Cup mentality is drudgery. It is hard! This is how dead religion feels—lifeless, like a lot of work.

On that day, however, Jesus had something greater than a cup mentality in mind for this woman. After ministering to her, He told her,

> Whoever drinks of this water will thirst again, but whoever drinks of the water that I shall give him will never thirst. But the water that I shall give him will become in him a fountain of water springing up into everlasting life.
>
> John 4:13–14

Jesus told her that day—and tells us now—about the living water. Just as the woman at the well discovered, we do not ever have to thirst again. The well lives within us. In the Old Testament, salvation was a cup, but now it is a well. What are you settling for? Are you a cup-carrying believer? Or are you tapping into the well?

Not long after giving my life to the Lord, I became thirsty for the things of God. One Sunday after church, I left the service feeling dissatisfied and frustrated. I decided to skip lunch (a big deal!) and go to the ocean to talk to the Lord. As I was crying out to God, I looked down to the water and saw a clear plastic Dixie cup, cracked and broken. The next wave washed the cup onto the rocks next to me. I picked up the cup and was immediately reminded of what more than one great revivalist has been known to say: "Why settle for a cupful when the whole ocean is yours?"

As I held that broken cup in my hand and glanced at the ocean, I made a decision that I was done with the cup. I was going to tap into the well that God made available to us.

I speak all over the world and host Firenights throughout New England, and I can tell you, many believers still only have cups. They come to meetings with cups, go to work with cups and believe their salvation is just a cup. Unfortunately, if the cup mentality remains your mind-set, you will only ever have a cupful. God has made a well available to you.

While attending the Feast of Tabernacles in Jerusalem, Jesus stood up and cried out to the crowds, "If anyone thirsts, let him come to Me and drink. He who believes in Me, as the Scripture has said, out of his heart will flow rivers of living water" (John 7:37–38). One of the traditions of this particular feast was for the high priest to dip a cup into the Pool of Siloam, representing the forgiveness of sins. Containers of oil were also paraded in the streets. And among the din of people, Jesus cried out, "Come to Me and drink!" Not only did He invite them to drink, but He also declared that if they did, rivers of living water would then flow out of them.

It is time to make a decision to live generously. Outpouring is near, and your cup will not be enough. Tap into the well of living water within you, and never be thirsty again.

Living Surrendered

Believers today want a Christianity with very little surrender. People have traded in power for personalities and courage for convenience. Droves of American believers look for churches that require less and less of them. Anything that makes people feel uncomfortable must be "religion," or the person speaking (the pastor) must be angry or racist or feminist or whatever. This could not be further from the truth! So many Christians are calling condemnation what is actually conviction, that sweet drawing of the Holy Spirit for more holiness in our lives.

In Luke chapter 5, Jesus called the first disciples. He approached a group of fishermen, spoke life to them and called them to a greater purpose. Peter reluctantly responded, and then saw a mighty miracle. Jesus called him and the others to be "fishers of men," and in that moment, we watch before our eyes the very description of the proper response to outpouring:

> For he [Simon Peter] and all who were with him were astonished at the catch of fish which they had taken; and so also were James and John, the sons of Zebedee, who were partners with Simon. And Jesus said to Simon, "Do not be afraid. From now on you

will catch men." So when they had brought their boats to land, they forsook all and followed Him.

Luke 5:9–11

This is the greatest description of the natural response to true revival—"they forsook all and followed Him."

The Narrow Road

Our response to God must be the same as the disciples' response that day. As I said back in my introduction, if your only understanding of outpouring is the roof blowing off the place you are in, you might be missing out. Outpouring also looks like the floor you are standing on falling out from underneath you. The natural and appropriate response to God is *always* surrender. Only by the Spirit can we accomplish this total surrender, as a result of the power of God.

There has been a slow decline of believers experiencing the real power of the Holy Spirit, and it absolutely is related to the void of true surrender in our lives. As a result, we have become subject to this "anything goes, do whatever you want" Christianity. Churches are scared of losing people, so they change their message.

Jesus was not politically correct when He said, "I am the way, the truth, and the life. No one comes to the Father except through Me" (John 14:6). He was not seeker sensitive when He said, "Enter by the narrow gate; for wide is the gate and broad is the way that leads to destruction, and there are many who go in by it. Because narrow is the gate and difficult is the way which leads to life, and there are few who find it" (Matthew 7:13–14).

A narrow road! The way to life is a narrow road. That is such a contrast to the message being preached in most American churches today. If we are going to see an outpouring of the Spirit of God, we must surrender all. We have come as far as our current level of surrender will allow.

The disciples gave the correct response when they left every-thing to follow Jesus. They were not holding on to see how much they could still retain from their former lives. They did not want to live in the flesh anymore. Despite what your flesh wants to hear, every day is not a Saturday in Christianity. There is a cross to bear and a price to pay, and if we want to see the nations burning for God and an outpouring of the Spirit of God, it will cost us everything.

Many churches and ministries have faced the dilemma of wanting crowds and success, which they perceive as fruit. So instead of preaching truth and standing firm on the principles of God, they start to change their beliefs. They make sure they never offend anyone, and they turn their services into a produc-tion. And this is all because there is no *fire*.

Don't Change the Recipe

Coca-Cola may be one of the most recognized brands in the world. In the southern area of the United States, it is a staple of the everyday diet. In 1985, Coke was beginning to lose sales to Pepsi, their main rival brand. In a desperate attempt to better their sales, Coke did the unthinkable. After nearly one hundred years, they changed their recipe.

They called it the "New Coke," hoping to create excitement and boost sales. The opposite happened. Americans were out-raged. It was not unusual to see people dumping "New Coke" down the drains in city streets. National news covered the in-tense response, and even Pepsi's CEO sent a memo[1] to Pepsi's staff that became publicized:

April 21, 1985

To all Pepsi Bottlers and Pepsi-Cola Company personnel:
  It gives me great pleasure to offer each of you my hearti-est congratulations.

After 87 years of going at it eyeball to eyeball, the other guy just blinked.

Coca-Cola is withdrawing their products from the marketplace, and is reformulating brand Coke to be "more like Pepsi." Too bad Ripley's not around . . . he could have had a field day with this one.

There is no question the long-term market success of Pepsi has forced this move.

Everyone knows when something is right it doesn't need changing.

Maybe they finally realized what most of us have known for years: Pepsi tastes better than Coke.

Well, people in trouble tend to do desperate things . . . and we'll have to keep our eye on them.

But for now, I say victory is sweet, and we have earned a celebration. We're going to declare a holiday on Friday.

> *Enjoy!*
> *Best Regards,*
> *Roger Enrico, president*
> *and chief executive officer,*
> *Pepsi-Cola USA*

A *CBS News* article titled "30 Years Ago Today, Coca-Cola Made Its Worst Mistake" said this:

A poll showed that only 13 percent of soda drinkers liked the new Coke. The pop was a bust of epic proportions. Pepsi took full advantage by launching a commercial featuring a girl who asked: "Somebody out there tell me why Coke did it? Why did Coke change?"

Fans weren't upset—they were angry. So passionate were Coke drinkers that they launched grassroots campaigns across the country to force Coca-Cola to bring back the original Coke.

"It was the people against the corporation—only in America," reported CBS News' Bob Simon in 1985. "Coke said it was committed, so were the people. In California they collected signatures, in Seattle they set up a hotline."

One protest group in particular gained national attention. The "Old Cola Drinkers of America," headed by Gay Mullins, was relentless in its pursuit to have the original Coke return. They set up petitions, provided pins with new Coke crossed out, and spoke to the media about their mission.[2]

It goes without saying that after only ninety days, the pressure and outrage grew to such a level that Coke held a press conference and admitted defeat. They changed the formula back, realizing that you just don't mess with a recipe that works.

"Why are we talking about Coke?" you ask. Because just like Coke, Christians today are changing the recipe. We are walking away from what has always worked in shaping this world for God. We are standing on the shoulders of a generation of awakeners and martyrs who have gone before us, setting the stage for abundant living for all generations to come. Why are we trying to change it now?

When He was on earth, Jesus set the example of how to live life. Nothing has changed. He died and rose again, and now He lives in us. The mission is the same. We cannot change the formula. We must allow the Holy Spirit to move in our midst. Flee from worldly lusts and pursue heaven with a passion. It is time to cry out, *Lord, light the fire again!*

Reality of Truth

The reality about the truth is that even if it is unpopular, it is still the truth. It may not be popular to preach against sin, but the truth is that sin separates us from God. It may not be popular to talk about repentance and surrender, but the reality is that these are required in our daily life. They are the main qualifiers for breakthrough and revival. The formula has not changed. The recipe for revival has always been the same:

> If My people who are called by My name will humble themselves, and pray and seek My face, and turn from their wicked ways, then I will hear from heaven, and will forgive their sin and heal their land.
>
> 2 Chronicles 7:14

We cannot expect the promised healing of our land without the drastic pursuit of holiness and longing to be like God—turning from our wicked ways and embracing heaven. Truth is truth. Grace does not provide an excuse to sin. The purpose of grace is to empower us to live a holy life. Grace holds us to a higher standard than the Law. Grace empowers us and allows us to enter into God's purposes and promises. It is not painful to want to be clean. This is the natural response for someone who has touched heaven. Sin is sin, and we must desire to be clean to ascend His hill (see Psalm 24:3–5).

Recently, I have noticed a disturbing pattern invading the culture of believers in New England. Churches and ministries that were once known for God's power and presence have changed the formula. Seeker sensitivity has started to drive the purpose behind each new program and service. The priority has become pleasing people and avoiding offense at all costs. This new formula has backfired, and slowly believers are returning to the original recipe.

Almost every month, someone asks me to speak at a Bible school or in a church-planting course. They look to me as if I have an authority concerning church planting and growth, and people want the recipe. Truthfully, I do not have time to accept all their invitations, and it is not a matter of having the recipe. I wish people would realize how easy it is to access all that heaven has for us simply by surrendering. In my experience, if you want to plant a church, the formula is only three words long: *Build a fire!* Establish the fire on the altar and let the Lord build from there.

The church you attend probably has a great sound system, excellent lighting, new bathrooms, perhaps even a coffee bar and a bookstore. Those things are secondary to the fire. Does your church have a fire burning at the altar? Is the pastor preaching the Word with boldness? Do you see miracles? If the answer to those questions is no, then it is time to move on to a place where the fire is burning, or start a church and build your own fire.

The appearance of professionalism or production will not impact or impart. I am not saying that I do not believe in doing things with excellence, but most people settle for the feel of real. Recycling dead men's brains will not stand as a substitute for the anointing, either. We cannot just repeat a sermonette that has been explained to us in an academic setting and think that doing that alone will be effective. It is time to receive a fresh impartation of the Holy Spirit and surrender every area of our lives to Jesus.

What Did Jesus Say?

Surrendered lives submit to the will of God. When the disciples left everything and followed Jesus, they did not know where this journey would take them. They had no clue what would occur in the following years. They knew that there was a miracle worker in their midst, and that He could most certainly be the Christ. The full picture had not yet been painted, but they were on to something. The same principle applies to our lives today. God reveals only a small glimpse into His goodness and plan for our lives, and based on that little taste, we must say yes to whatever will happen next.

When I was young, we played a game called Simon Says. It is a simple game children have been playing for years. The person who is leading, or "Simon," asks participants to perform a series of motions or exercises. Anyone playing must do exactly what Simon says, but *only* if the leader begins his or her instructions with the phrase "Simon says . . ." For example, the leader states, "Simon says, 'Pat your head,'" and all the players should pat their heads. Then the leader quickly says, "Raise your hand!" Anyone who raises a hand is now out of the game, because Simon did not say it first.

The game is very simple; you listen carefully and do exactly what Simon says. I loved this game as a child, and I remember how intently I would listen so I would be able to stay in the game and perhaps even win a chance to be Simon myself. Unlike this game, Christianity seems to be the only religion where the followers are content with *not* doing what the Leader says. It is a broken system where believers have Scripture memorized but have no intention of doing what it says. We are content with singing songs of loyalty and love, but we walk out of the church and never do what we sang about only moments before.

The staff members at our ministry are all people who were touched by God's fire and then were called to serve faithfully in our churches. They really love and support the dream God has given Debbie and me. We are blessed with committed people who know our hearts and work hard to help create the vision God has given us. My assistant in particular is one who knows the ins and outs of every working part of the ministry and is someone my wife and I trust wholeheartedly.

With that in mind, imagine with me this scenario: EHC is hosting a large conference, and a couple of national guest speakers are coming to the church to minister. We are expecting to host a large crowd of people for this event. I am about to meet with my assistant and ask her to go over our checklists before the conference so we can mobilize staff and volunteers to usher, clean, host guests, work book tables, organize parking and carry out the many other details that make a large event like this happen. I notice some trash in the nursery moments before coming into our meeting, so I additionally mention to her that the trash needs to be removed as soon as possible. Her immediate response is, "Yes, Pastor, I'll make sure we get it now."

The following day when I arrive at EHC, I glance at the nursery and see the same trash that I had asked her to remove the day before. This confuses me, so I search for my assistant to discuss the issue. When I find her, she is sitting around a conference table with some other people. I mention to her what I saw: "I just walked by the trash in the nursery again, and it has not been removed. Can you tell me why?"

She looks at me and says, "Yes, Pastor. I heard you yesterday, and we are all meeting right now to go over your request and study my notes on what you said."

I find this strange, but I leave the meeting, trusting it will be done because she says it will be done.

The next day, I walk into the church, glance at the nursery and once again see the same trash. I am pretty upset at this point. I go straight to the office to find my assistant and confront her about why the trash is still there. This time, I find not only my assistant, but also my entire staff in the office. They are singing songs about the trash removal. I am beyond frustrated. My very small, simple request is left undone while they have held studies about it, memorized the mandate and even written songs about the request. They have done everything but take out the trash!

Today, this nation is filled with believers holding Bible studies, singing songs, creating YouTube videos, but not doing what Jesus said. Did "Jesus say"? Then do exactly that! We all know that witnessing to the lost and seeing souls saved is the will of God, so it shocks me how many people will do everything else but share their faith.

In Luke 9:1–2, Jesus gave His disciples power and authority: "Then He called His twelve disciples together and gave them power and authority over all demons, and to cure diseases. He sent them to preach the kingdom of God and to heal the sick." That power was not given so we could sing songs about a miracle-working God. That authority was not given so we could post on Facebook about His power. Our actions declare our beliefs and, ultimately, our level of surrender:

> For I will not dare to speak of any of those things which Christ has not accomplished through me, in word and deed, to make the Gentiles obedient—in mighty signs and wonders, by the power of the Spirit of God, so that from Jerusalem and round about to Illyricum I have fully preached the gospel of Christ. And so I have made it my aim to preach the gospel, not where Christ was named . . .
>
> Romans 15:18–20

Those who believe and administer the Gospel do so "in word and deed." True surrender to God's will brings change and gives feet to our words and beliefs.

Take a Towel

God's Son, Jesus Christ, perfectly and beautifully exemplified this message of surrender. He lived His life on this earth as a road map for our lives. At the end of His time on earth, He had loved His friends "to the end."

> Now before the Feast of the Passover, when Jesus knew that His hour had come that He should depart from this world to the Father, having loved His own who were in the world, He loved them to the end.
>
> John 13:1

It is in the moments of praise and power that we see who people really are. Are you surrendered? Or are you after your own attention and gain? Let's see what Jesus did in His final moment of power:

> Jesus, knowing that the Father had given all things into His hands, and that He had come from God and was going to God, rose from supper and laid aside His garments, took a towel and girded Himself. After that, He poured water into a basin and began to wash the disciples' feet, and to wipe them with the towel with which He was girded.
>
> John 13:3–5

Jesus finished strong. He was fully aware of the gravity of that moment, and He grabbed a towel to serve and love the ones who had been sent to Him as friends while He walked the earth. This is a leadership model you do not often see today. One of the greatest dangers in our journey with God is becoming impressed with ourselves. Jesus modeled the heart of the Kingdom of God in this moment. He modeled what a surrendered life truly looks like.

Identity is knowing who you are. Purpose is knowing what you are called to do. When we continually remain in a posture of surrender, we lock ourselves into identity and purpose. A surrendered life clarifies both of these things for the believer. We must live in the fire and allow it to burn away everything that is not from God. We know by this Scripture we just read that Jesus had unlimited resources. "The Father had given all things into His hands," and we see His position of surrender and service.

In 2 Peter 1:3, it says that He has given all things to us. In the same manner we must give all things to Him, continuing to live a life of surrender, making room for the outpouring of the Spirit of God. You will not experience all that God has for you by fighting. It can only be received, like a child.

If you are serving to receive affirmation, or if you help others for personal gain, that is not a heart of surrender. The difference between what is in your account in heaven and what is in your possession on this earth is directly connected to surrender. Serving is at the heart of surrender. Authentic Christianity is really about a surrendered Servant-King who came to wash His friends' feet. This is in great contrast to what we see in churches today. Most believers are not serving from surrendered hearts, and the world can discern that. It repels them rather than drawing them in.

What if we filled our cities with surrendered servants? What if we loved to the point of killing the flesh? What if our breakthrough was directly connected to our surrendered heart toward God? What if our churches across the world really had spiritual power, and personal gain was not at the root of it? That is the beginning of awakening.

The Way In

When you became a Christian, what was the reason? Was your heart convicted? Did someone invite you to a Bible study or a church service? Or perhaps you had an encounter with God alone. People meet Jesus under many different circumstances. Whatever the situation, I can guarantee this: No one ever came to Jesus because of pride.

Nobody becomes a Christian because he or she has a lot of money in the bank and wants to thank someone. People do not encounter God because they hit the lotto and want to show their gratitude by giving it away. People do not become born again because they are so famous and are recognized by so many people that they realize there is a God out there other than them.

No, it is the exact opposite. We come to Jesus because we are broken and in need of a Savior. We encounter God because we understand that we are sinners and need to be saved from ourselves. We encounter His love and receive forgiveness. We become new creations because of what He paid for at Calvary. We owed a debt we could not pay, and that blood was shed for our forgiveness and freedom.

John Wimber, an iconic figure in recent Christian history, would often say, "The way in is the way on." Meaning this: The way we came to Jesus is how we continue to advance and grow with God. Surrendered. Broken. In need of a Savior. The same spiritual posture we had when we came to God must remain our posture to the very end. This is the way to advance and fulfill God's purpose in and through our lives.

Surrendered hearts will always see awakening. There is coming a great outpouring of the Spirit of God unlike this earth has seen. Will you make room for it? Are you willing to let go of who you are, for all that He is? I believe that as we surrender, we prepare a place for God to dwell, and we become the vessel He will use.

Expect to live for Jesus like never before. Go grab a towel!

Living a Life
That Worships

When God touches a person, there is a tangible and obvious response. Whether it is a person who sings like an angel or a person who cannot carry a tune in a bucket, people all do the same thing when they begin to burn for God—they *worship*.

I believe one of the most misunderstood passions in the Church is worship. It is not about a platform or an instrument. It is about a heart that is earnestly chasing God. I believe with all my heart that the next great outpouring will be marked by worship.

To really understand the power of worship, we have to go back to the very beginning. All the angels in heaven had assignments, and there was one angel in particular who was highly ranked. He was named Lucifer, "son of the morning." And it was Lucifer, soon to be known as Satan, our great adversary, who was the first worship leader. The Scripture says of him, "The workmanship of your timbrels and pipes was prepared for you on the day you were created" (Ezekiel 28:13).

If Satan was a worship leader in heaven, then we can clearly see the power of worship here on this earth. It is no wonder that this is an area of our personal Christian experience that is consistently under attack. Satan knows the power of worship. Every time God moves in power, it is always marked with worship. True worship changes everything. Worship will draw a line in the sand. It will cause you to make a choice between receiving breakthrough and living in bondage.

One definition of worship is "to honor or reverence as a divine being."[1] Whatever you consider your source or your savior is what you will worship. Some people worship money, and that is their god. Some people worship reputation, and that is their idol. Satan knows the power of worship, and it was when he stopped worshiping that he lost his position in heaven:

> How you have fallen from heaven, O star of the morning, son of the dawn! You have been cut down to the earth, you who have weakened the nations! But you said in your heart, "I will ascend to heaven; I will raise my throne above the stars of God, and I will sit on the mount of assembly in the recesses of the north. I will ascend above the heights of the clouds; I will make myself like the Most High." Nevertheless you will be thrust down to Sheol, to the recesses of the pit.
>
> Isaiah 14:12–15 NASB

Yes, when you are thinking too highly of *you*, it will allow a seed to come in and cause disruption to the movement of God. That is what happened to Satan. Today it is no different; we must all watch out for that mind-set that separates and divides.

A Change in the Atmosphere

Worship has the power to change your circumstances. Worship changes your atmosphere. Many believe worship is only about God. And, yes, while God is worthy of all of our worship, He does not *need* our worship. God is not confused or insecure about who He is. When we worship God, He remains the same, but *we* are changed. When we worship, we take our eyes and our minds off our own surroundings. Worship brings into focus what truly matters—God's presence in our lives. And when a fresh outpouring comes on the Body of Christ, it will be marked by worship.

God longs to see our world and our wills shaped by our determination to exalt Him no matter what the circumstances. When our hearts are tuned to give Him praise in adversity, we become a people who exalt God based on who He is, not on what we are facing at that particular moment. Worship is a very natural expression of whatever it is we most value.

I remember being at a Justin Bieber concert a few years ago with Justin's mom, Pattie Mallette. As we were looking out at an ocean of young girls screaming and crying, some of them overwhelmed even to the point of passing out, I turned to her and asked, "What goes through your mind when you see people acting this way?"

And she did not miss a beat with her answer: "It shows me that we were created to worship."

Worship is a natural instinct placed inside each one of us by God Himself. Everybody worships. The question is, *What* do you worship? We cannot find the true meaning and freedom behind it until we worship Jesus. God designed worship so that we could find our fullest expression in life through thanksgiving, praise and worship.

The gospel of John, chapter 4, records the account of Jesus meeting a woman at a well in Samaria. After many attempts on His part to explain to her what God's desire for worship is, Jesus made an amazing statement: "God is Spirit, and those who worship Him must worship in spirit and truth" (verse 24).

Jesus did *not* say God is looking for worship. God is looking for *worshipers*. Every plan God has ever established on this earth is motivated by love. And if God chose us to be worshipers, then that means God designed worship to have an effect on us. You are a worshiper. And the Father has been clear that He is looking for worshipers. He is looking for *you*.

God is also looking for worshipers who worship with purity—not with manipulation or with desire for ill-gotten gain or with ulterior motives. Worship is not a means to an end. It is *the end*. It is exactly what we were created for. God chose to design us to worship for one simple reason—we become like what we worship.

There is no greater passion God could have but that we would be conformed into the image of Jesus. There is a Scripture that explains this to us: "Beloved, now we are children of God; and it has not yet been revealed what we shall be, but we know that when He is revealed, we shall be like Him, for we shall see Him as He is" (1 John 3:2).

What you behold, you become like. I have seen people love and serve God for thirty years. They attend church and live as faithfully as they can, but the only worship experience they have is for twenty minutes on a Sunday once a week. On the other hand, I have also seen people get saved on the streets and then cry out to God and worship for hours a day privately because they are so in love with Jesus. The person who was saved on the streets and worships for hours every day will, after two years, bear the image of God more than the thirty-year saint who is not much of a worshiper, for one reason alone—*worship matters*.

If your only worship experience is on Sunday morning, I question if you truly have met Jesus. We are transformed by our exposure to His glory. Worship transforms us. Every time you take time to worship the Lord, you are being changed.

Thanksgiving, Praise and Worship

There are three main expressions in the Bible when it comes to being a worshiper of God: thanksgiving, praise and worship itself. Look at how Psalm 100:3–5 begins to describe them:

Know that the LORD, He is God; it is He who has made us, and not we ourselves; we are His people and the sheep of His pasture. Enter into His gates with thanksgiving, and into His courts with praise. Be thankful to Him, and bless His name. For the LORD is good; His mercy is everlasting, and His truth endures to all generations.

Although there would not be enough pages in one hundred different books to cover our different expressions of worship properly, I will do my best to lay a basic foundation for you as we look at these three main expressions more closely.

Thanksgiving

Thanksgiving is our response to the acts of God. It is our recognition of what He has done. It is not just having a thankful heart, but also opening our mouths and giving Him the recognition. Thankfulness is meant to be verbally expressed. We have to open our mouths and give Him thanks.

"Give thanks in all circumstances; for this is God's will for you in Christ Jesus," 1 Thessalonians 5:18 (NIV) tells us. It is the Father's desire that we express our thanksgiving. We have to look back and give thanks for what He has done, and also look ahead and give thanks for what He will do. Thanksgiving is the entryway to understanding His nature. Thanking Him for His righteous acts is essential, a starting point for worship—grade 1, the ABCs and 1-2-3s.

It is not enough to be acquainted only with His acts—we must know His ways. Understanding His acts will lead us to the place of knowing Him. Moses even prayed, "Lord, show me your ways" (see Exodus 33:13). If we truly knew what God was like, we would never lock the doors of our churches. We must know His ways, and we therefore enter His gates with thanksgiving, that we might know Him more.

Praise

Thanksgiving will always lead us to an overwhelming desire to know who God is, and this overwhelming desire is called *praise*. Praise comes after thanksgiving. It is the joyful declaration of all that God has done for us. It is closely intertwined with thanksgiving, as we offer back to God our appreciation for His mighty works on our behalf.

Praise is universal and can be applied to other relationships as well. We can praise our family, friends, boss or pastor. Praise does not require anything of us. It is merely the truthful acknowledgment of the righteous acts of another. It is an outward expression of good. Since God has done many wonderful deeds, He is worthy of praise (see Psalm 18:3).

Praise is also a sacrifice. It is mentioned all throughout the Bible as a command and an instruction for believers. After we give thanks for what God has done, we start to recognize who He is. That is when praise begins. We start to cry out expressively and acknowledge His nature.

Praise is often referred to as the "sacrifice of praise." When you face trials or hardships, praise is your weapon. It is your access to deeper places. Praise really transforms us as we offer it as a sacrifice to the Lord. Praise will not always involve a feeling, because it is meant to kill the flesh in many ways.

Worship

Worship is the next step after praise. We can give thanksgiving and praise every time we are together, but worship is not always present. It is possible to celebrate someone whom you have not drawn near to, but worship goes beyond that. Worship is the "nearer still" exchange of our experience with God's presence.

In the Old Testament, the words used for worship can be pictured as "bowing low." In the New Testament, the words for worship are connected to the word *kiss*. God is such a lover that He looks for worship.

Worship is the final and deepest exchange. Worship is very different from thanksgiving and praise. Thanksgiving is giving thanks and acknowledging God's ways. Praise is a sacrifice and is done whether you feel like it or not. It is an offering of praise—no matter what. Worship, unlike praise, is where you *become* the sacrifice. It is about His presence. It is deep, and it is full of surrender and abandonment and passion and love. "Yet a time is coming and has now come when the true worshipers will worship the Father in the Spirit and in truth, for they are the kind of worshipers the Father seeks" (John 4:23 NIV).

Worship leader Jason Upton posted this recently on one of his social media accounts: "There are a host of worship leaders that help direct my attention to the presence of Jesus daily, and only a few of them play music."[2]

Worship is about God's presence. In worship, we allow His presence to overtake our lives. Worship and His presence really must be seen as one thing. It is His presence that transforms us. And you *feel* that. You allow it to wreck you, to change you. You must be aware of His presence and make a life practice of worshiping Jesus. You will always reflect the realm of which you are most aware.

Christianity today is shallow. There is very little depth to our devotion. Christianity was never meant to be a club or classroom. It is meant to be an exchange, an intimacy that leaves us undone and changes the world around us. I have had encounters with angels, true angelic visitations. Though I have only experienced this a handful of times, every single time these encounters have left me undone and have shaken the world around me. These visitations were accompanied by notable miracles, new levels in my understanding of God and souls. Lots and lots of souls.

Church "doesn't work" for many people because they *are not worshiping*. Attending a Sunday service today can be like walking into a theater, a circus of well-dressed performance preachers. If you are not touching heaven during church, then why would you want to go? It has turned into a show. We were not meant to assemble together to watch a movie. This is not Hollywood! Worship has to be about becoming the sacrifice, lying down on the altar and allowing God to change you.

Thanksgiving, praise and worship are all different expressions of how we worship God, and all three have their place. In thanksgiving, we respond to what He has done. In praise, we acknowledge who He is, which is considered a sacrifice. And finally, in worship, we *become* the sacrifice. We become the offering.

What Are You Reflecting?

"But we all, with unveiled face, beholding as in a mirror the glory of the Lord, are being transformed into the same image from glory to glory, just as by the Spirit of the Lord" (2 Corinthians 3:18). True worship is a mirror. It transforms us into the image of Jesus.

Many years ago, I was out running errands after an intense and prolonged time of prayer and worship in the morning. While I was out, I wanted to stop by the house of a childhood friend to see how he was doing. His home was in a rougher area of the city, similar to where we grew up. We stood on the porch together, talking and catching up with one another. At the time, this friend was in a difficult place and was very discouraged. I will never forget how, as I was encouraging him and testifying to him about all that God had done for me, another man whom I had never seen before approached us on the steps.

My friend called out to him, "What's up, man!"

It seemed as if they were familiar with each other, but immediately the man shouted, "No! I'm not here to talk to you!" Then he shifted his eyes to me, pointed his finger in my face and said, "*You*, on the other hand. I can see the very glory of

God upon you! As I was walking by, I felt power on you, as if you were Jesus Himself!"

This man was not a Christian. He did not know Jesus. And yet he knew that when he felt the power around me, he wanted to be free. He went on to tell me that he had fought in the Vietnam War and had to kill people to stay alive. He felt as though God would never forgive him, and he had been running from God for years.

I shared the Gospel with him and prayed for him. He gave his life to Jesus for the first time and was filled with the Holy Spirit. On the porch, with my friend standing there, this man was miraculously delivered and began speaking in tongues.

This story is not about me. This is about the power of worship. I had just come out of intense worship before visiting my friend, and it had transformed me more into the image of Jesus, which is what the man walking by noticed in me. We become different people when we worship. I am a different person when I am in His presence. His power transforms us. And the devil knows it.

Let's clear up some things about worship. It is possible to go to church and not worship. You can be a Christian and never reflect the glory of God. Satan knows this and wants to keep us away from being transformed. The majority of American believers are full of their flesh. Less is getting accomplished here on the earth because America is a third-world nation spiritually, and it is directly connected to a lack of worship. The percentage of Christians in America has not changed. The percentage of Christians *engaging heaven* is nearly nonexistent. Trust me, it shows.

In the prophetic church culture I see as I travel around the world and speak in churches heavily focused on the prophetic (which I love), people approach me regularly to tell me about their angelic visions, prophecies and words from the Lord. Here is the problem: I cannot feel heaven on many of them because they look like hell; it is so obvious that they are not in God's presence, not worshiping. Their experiences are full of flesh and are ineffective. Satan *loves* this and wants it to continue.

Worry or Worship?

Do you want to end worry? *Worship!* Many Christians are overcome with worry and depression, living anxious and on edge. This is the deficit left by a lack of worship in our lives. You cannot worry and worship at the same time. You must choose one or the other. Problems appear to be bigger than God without worship, but when you are in His presence, your problems shrink down to size. When you spend too much time in your own presence, problems bloat and distort, appearing larger than they actually are. Believers should not be weighed down with the affairs of this world. We are destined to be worshiping warriors:

> No one engaged in warfare entangles himself with the affairs of this life, that he may please him who enlisted him as a soldier. And also if anyone competes in athletics, he is not crowned unless he competes according to the rules. The hardworking farmer must be first to partake of the crops. Consider what I say, and may the Lord give you understanding in all things.
>
> 2 Timothy 2:4–7

We cannot afford to get entangled with this world. This world has nothing for us anyway. It is only temporary. We cannot become too attached to this fading place. Worship protects us from getting entangled. When we find ourselves tangled by the weeds of this world, worship changes that and opens up our "understanding in all things." We find discernment when we spend time in God's presence.

"Oh, magnify the LORD with me, and let us exalt His name together" (Psalm 34:3). What a powerful verse! God is magnified when we worship. This does not mean that God actually becomes bigger as we worship. He is always the same. This means that, as we worship, He becomes bigger *to us*. Worship changes our perception of the size of our God.

I have amazing news for you today: As you worship, God will become larger in your life. You do not even have to come with a laundry list of concerns. When you get into His presence, your list disappears. And if anything remains, He will give you the strength and wisdom you need to know exactly how to handle each and every situation.

Peace

Where has peace gone? It seems that there are so few people who actually have peace. God's peace is a gift for believers that is not even available to this world: "Peace I leave with you, My peace I give to you; not as the world gives do I give to you. Let not your heart be troubled, neither let it be afraid" (John 14:27).

The world does not have true peace. People in and of the world have to strive for it, but believers do not need to strive. It does not need to be strived for, just received. Peace is our inheritance, our anchor.

I watch believers today attempt to obtain peace outside God's presence. It will never happen. Peace is not the absence of conflict, but the presence of a Person. We receive perfect peace in worship. Once you have experienced peace in His presence, you value it and hold it dear. We cannot have strong families without worship and peace. We will not be able to make decisions properly without our "decision maker," which is peace.

I encourage and challenge you today—*worship!* Put this book down *now* and get on your face. I will still be here when you are done. Allow the power of God to invade your life. Become the sacrifice today. And when you do that, I believe you will see Jeremiah 33:3 happen in full form: "Call to Me, and I will answer you, and show you great and mighty things, which you do not know." Get ready for the unknown!

Never Forgetting the Purpose

Take a moment to imagine that you are a member of the original twelve disciples. You have not read the New Testament because it does not exist yet, because *you are the New Testament.* You do not see or even comprehend the whole picture of what is about to happen on the earth. All you know is that for the past three years, this man called the Christ has radically transformed your life. He has performed miracles, taught you and rebuked you. He has shown you who the Father is.

Then you stood by as He was wrongly arrested, falsely accused and sentenced, beaten and tortured, and murdered brutally on a cross. And beyond that, you have seen with your own eyes that He miraculously came back to life, walking and talking among you again. You have experienced the worst possible scenario you could have imagined. You lost the one thing in your life that actually mattered—the thing you left everyone and everything you loved behind for—and then, by the grace and power of God, He has returned to you.

Early one morning, Jesus wakes you and your fellow companions and asks you to follow Him to Bethany, a village on the Mount of Olives. As usual, you are unsure about what is going to happen on this trip—you just know that He has asked you to go and that you have committed to follow Him. He once mentioned leaving to prepare a place in heaven for you. You are sad at the idea of Him going. You have already lost Him once. You have grown to love Jesus so much, how can you live a day without Him? But you know He has a plan. You are never quite sure what it is, but somehow, you are important to Him. He is going to use you on the earth to do mighty things when He is gone.

Once you and your party arrive at the Mount of Olives, He gathers you around Himself and begins to give what seems to be departing statements. You know in your heart that this is it. He is really going this time. Here is Mark's account of this very moment. (I know we looked at part of this same passage back in principle #3, but this time remember to imagine you are actually there):

> Later He appeared to the eleven as they sat at the table; and He rebuked their unbelief and hardness of heart, because they did not believe those who had seen Him after He had risen. And He said to them, "Go into all the world and preach the gospel to every creature. He who believes and is baptized will be saved; but he who does not believe will be condemned. And these signs will follow those who believe: In My name they will cast out demons; they will speak with new tongues; they will take up serpents; and if they drink anything deadly, it will by no means hurt them; they will lay hands on the sick, and they will recover."
>
> So then, after the Lord had spoken to them, He was received up into heaven, and sat down at the right hand of God.
>
> Mark 16:14–19

Jesus sums up three years of mentoring with a few charges and final thoughts, and then *boom*, He is gone. There is no time to ask questions, no time to think. You and your friends stand there, mouths open, hearts heavy, shocked by the realization that He is not here anymore. This is one of the greatest moments to occur in the history of humanity, and you are there to witness it. Tears, wonder, concern, anticipation—there is no possible way at that moment to measure the full magnitude of it.

The memories of the last three years pass before your eyes like a flash—miracles, teaching, multitudes, death, resurrection, new life. And now He is gone. What you do with this moment will determine the course of history. He has entrusted you to take His message to the ends of the earth.

In His final moment with His best friends, Jesus is straightforward and to the point, as He always was. He asks you to preach, baptize people and heal the sick. He also says He will always protect you in the process. And that is it. Now it is done. He is gone, and you are here.

You are here!

And here is my question: What do you do with that moment? Suppose someone blurts out, "What do we do now?" What is your response?

Believers today would probably want to go over what the mandate was several thousand times. We would want to consider everyone's opinion of the situation and form a "What Now?" list. We might package up the dirt where it all happened and sell it as "Ascension Dirt" to make money to support His command. Or how about we just build little communities called "churches" and leave it at that?

What was the response of the early Church after witnessing something so powerful?

> And they went out and preached everywhere, the Lord working with them and confirming the word through the accompanying signs. Amen.
>
> Mark 16:20

Yes! This is the proper response—evangelism and power!

How we have gotten so far from this is beyond me. Jesus died so we could live life like *He* lived life. We are meant to shape the world around us. The Kingdom of God is at our disposal. We were created to release the fire and the power of God. We were created to heal the sick. We were created to be demon masters.

Miracle Mandate

It is widely accepted by charismatic believers that miracles are for today, but so many have given up on the idea that they can see miracles through their lives right now. Miracles are always for someone else. The idea of needing miracles is less of a mandate and more of a last-ditch effort. This was never meant to be the case. It is the opposite, in fact. It is next to impossible to learn how to believe for miracles, signs and wonders during moments of trial and trauma. This is something that must be lived daily as we pursue God.

Our God is a God of miracles, signs and wonders, the greatest of these always being the salvation of the sinner. When Jesus lived on this earth, He had a mandate: "seek and save that which is lost." Our ministry, EHC, works regularly with those in life whom many would call down-and-out—people who sleep on the streets, dealing with addictions of all kinds. And every time we see someone transformed, it is nothing short of glorious. It is a wonder to watch someone who is not regularly churched get transformed and become passionate for God. People like that just do not know any different, so they pick up the Word of God and then they obey it.

It should be the natural experience of a believer to witness and see miracles regularly. If you are not seeing that in your life, then it is time to come back to your first love and encounter Jesus again. Pick up the Word of God and obey it. God has established a partnership with us. He now lives in us, and the mandate never changed. We just get to be part of it now.

One of the main purposes of the second chapter of Acts is to communicate clearly our miracle mandate. It is there (and in other places in the book of Acts as well) that we find the word *witness*. And that is what we are. Witnesses.

Why did Jesus, the Son of God, choose to die and leave us as the dwelling places for the Holy Spirit to abide? Take a moment to ponder that concept—Jesus died and has now resurrected Himself *in us*! Why? Because we will need that much power for the task that is ahead of us.

When we see this coming outpouring of the Spirit of God, it is *not* so the Church can have extra meetings and roll around on the floor, although that may be part of it. An outpouring of the Spirit of God is for the *lost to be saved*, for Christians to be revived and for lives to be transformed.

I spent a good portion of my previous book, *Revival Hunger* (Destiny Image, 2011), talking about hungering and thirsting for God. Some professors and theologians were offended by the title of the book, and the summary of their offense was this: "The use of the word *revival* assumes that something has died. It assumes that something is not alive."

Yes. Exactly.

Awakening is a term used for unbelievers, those who have not yet confessed that Jesus is Lord. When awakening falls, it is a "God-awareness" falling on a city, with the lost being saved in droves. *Revival* is a Church-only experience. Those who are lost—the unbelievers—cannot be revived, because there was no prior state of life in them. We are dead in our sin without a belief in Christ, the Son of the living God. *Outpouring* is all of the above. It is the hearts of believers being revived again, and awakening falling on the nations of the earth. It is a blanket outpouring of the Spirit of God, with no respect as to who, what, when, where or why.

Abiding

The Lord has shown me that we are going to experience a fresh wave of fire moving through our lives, resulting in a renewed passion for the lost. It is going to come through a deep level of abiding in His presence. I am convinced that the lack of soul-winning and miracles in America is directly connected to a lack of abiding in Christ. When outpouring hits our land, believers are going to be filled up to the point of bubbling over and spilling out everywhere they go.

We have to keep in mind that it is Jesus who is the standard, not the pastor at the dead church you grew up in. Jesus is the example of how we are to live our lives, not *any* man. People will always fall short. We must stop aiming so low. *Study Jesus.* How was He motivated, what did He say, what did He do? *Do that.* How did He approach demons? *Do the same.* What kind of confidence did He have? On whom did He show mercy? *Do that, do that, do that!*

Let's look at a passage of Scripture that is so powerful yet has been misquoted and misinterpreted for years. In Mark 9:17–29, a father whose son had a demon spirit that was causing seizures and erratic behavior approached Jesus for help:

> Then one of the crowd answered and said, "Teacher, I brought You my son, who has a mute spirit. And wherever it seizes him, it throws him down; he foams at the mouth, gnashes his teeth, and becomes rigid. So I spoke to Your disciples, that they should cast it out, but they could not."
>
> He answered him and said, "O faithless generation, how long shall I be with you? How long shall I bear with you? Bring him to Me." Then they brought him to Him. And when he saw Him, immediately the spirit convulsed him, and he fell on the ground and wallowed, foaming at the mouth.
>
> So He asked his father, "How long has this been happening to him?"

And he said, "From childhood. And often he has thrown him both into the fire and into the water to destroy him. But if You can do anything, have compassion on us and help us."

Jesus said to him, "If you can believe, all things are possible to him who believes."

Immediately the father of the child cried out and said with tears, "Lord, I believe; help my unbelief!"

When Jesus saw that the people came running together, He rebuked the unclean spirit, saying to it, "Deaf and dumb spirit, I command you, come out of him and enter him no more!" Then the spirit cried out, convulsed him greatly, and came out of him. And he became as one dead, so that many said, "He is dead." But Jesus took him by the hand and lifted him up, and he arose.

And when He had come into the house, His disciples asked Him privately, "Why could we not cast it out?"

So He said to them, "This kind can come out by nothing but prayer and fasting."

Jesus asked this father a question about belief, and then He said, "Deaf and dumb spirit, I command you, come out of him and enter him no more!"

Wow, can you imagine witnessing this? What power! What authority! Jesus was the Son of God, come to earth to dominate devils, and in the moment, not a single person doubted it.

It has been a habit of the Church to read this Scripture and automatically side with the unbelief of the disciples. The father approached them first, but they could do nothing to help. When the disciples asked Jesus privately why they could not cast out the demon, Jesus responded, "This kind can come out by nothing but prayer and fasting."

The interesting part of this is that we never once see a recorded biblical account of Jesus fasting for a demon to be cast out of a person. And Jesus is the standard, right? He is always the example. If we do not see Jesus fasting for a specific demon, then we should not have to do that.

If you are not defeating demons when you encounter them, in the moment is not the time to fast and pray for a specific demon. That is not what Jesus meant. Jesus was teaching us about abiding in the Father, with prayer and fasting included regularly in our pursuit of Him. What He said was about *abiding in Christ*. When you have a deep relationship with God, then when you face these kinds of devils, you *will* see them expelled.

God is in charge, but He is not in control. He has left the willingness up to us. Ephesians 3:20 says this: "Now to Him who is able to do exceedingly abundantly above all that we ask or think, according to the power that works in us."

According to the power that works in us. This phrase is what we call a disclaimer. Who controls the amount of power we experience in our lives? You and I do. God created a partnership between Jesus and us as believers so we can manifest His dominion on this earth. That is why fasting and prayer are so important. God's hands are not tied—*yours are.* Through abiding and agreement, we must partner with His will on this earth. He wants to move through you.

Let's look at another passage that has often been misunderstood:

> Now it happened, on a certain day, that He got into a boat with His disciples. And He said to them, "Let us cross over to the other side of the lake." And they launched out. But as they sailed He fell asleep. And a windstorm came down on the lake, and they were filling with water, and were in jeopardy. And they came to Him and awoke Him, saying, "Master, Master, we are perishing!"
>
> Then He arose and rebuked the wind and the raging of the water. And they ceased, and there was a calm. But He said to them, "Where is your faith?"
>
> And they were afraid, and marveled, saying to one another, "Who can this be? For He commands even the winds and water, and they obey Him!"
>
> Luke 8:22–25

If Peter had been a member of a standard American church today, he would have approached the pastor or even the entire congregation and shared this story with them. And they would have called him courageous: "Wow, Peter, what an answer to prayer!"

Can we talk about what Jesus called it? *Unbelief.*

This is a "testimony" that would be applauded in most churches of our time. Jesus' response was, "Where is your faith?"

Have you ever attempted to start your car, only then to realize you have forgotten your keys? You may have even opened the garage and then sat in the car for a moment, preparing for your drive. But you did not realize that your keys were not with you until you needed them. In moments like these, we do not wonder if we have a set of keys or not. We *have* the keys. We just did not *bring the keys with us*. Solving this problem is a simple matter of getting the keys from wherever they are so you can start your car.

When Jesus asked the disciples where their faith was, He was not wondering out loud if they had lost it in the raging sea around them. He was not saying they did not *have* faith, only that they did not *use the faith they had in their possession in that moment.*

Sometimes God wants to do things *through* you and not *for* you. Jesus transformed the wind and waves, but not before hinting that the disciples should have done it themselves. When Jesus silenced that storm, He was just showing them what was inside Him (and inside them)—the Kingdom within, manifested on the outside. He spoke peace from a place of peace. He declared healing from a place of healing.

We all know "that" person—the one who can control the whole room with his or her anger. Such people do not have to say anything, yet the whole room picks up on their attitude and then begins manifesting it. What is happening is that the inner anger and venom of those people are controlling the atmosphere around them and affecting their surroundings. Whatever is on the inside of you will manifest on the outside of you. It is a natural process. You will reflect what is in your heart in any circumstance, especially in times of pressure and frustration.

It is typical for believers only to manifest the conditions around them. It is the design of the Father, however, that believers be those people who demonstrate the Kingdom within, so that everywhere they go, it reflects and manifests around them. The beauty of this approach is that you get to control it. You are the gatekeeper of your surroundings instead of remaining a victim to every wind and wave around you.

Renewed Heart

"Keep your heart with all diligence, for out of it spring the issues of life" (Proverbs 4:23). We have to learn to guard our hearts, because whatever is in there will come out eventually. If we are going to see the miraculous demonstrated from our lives, it will only be from a place of victory and healing.

The Kingdom of God is the world in reverse. To live, you must first die. To go higher, you must first go lower. To a renewed mind and heart, the impossible is logical. We are called to summon the unseen realm to this earth. We are believers first, not feelers. We are created for signs and wonders. We are called to release this fire to a lost and dying world.

When the fire of God transforms us, we become qualified for an unending flame. We received the power in the moment of the original disciples' commission. Now it is time to live up to the high calling we have in Christ Jesus.

Napoleon Bonaparte was general of a mighty army and was one of the greatest military minds in history. One day, he met another soldier who was also named Napoleon. This soldier, however, was very timid and too nervous to fight. It is recorded that on one occasion the general looked at the young soldier with his same name and exclaimed, "Son, you better change your name or live up to it!"

It is time that we as believers do the same. It is time to redefine the name *Christian* that we carry in our nation and around the world. The tide is turning, and change is coming. Believers who have walked away from their roots are beginning to turn back. People are desperate for the power of God, and when people are desperate, things start changing. You will be part of this end-time army.

Turning Back

The Full Gospel Business Men's Fellowship (FGBMF) is an organization I have been involved with for years, and I have always loved being connected to it. In the 1980s, President Ronald Reagan said that there was no greater Christian organization in America than the FGBMF. Robert Bignold, who is now with the Lord, was the national president of the FGBMF for many years. He was a powerful figure in my life, a sold-out, on-fire Christian businessman whom God sent to my wife and me to teach us many valuable lessons in the early years of our marriage.

A few years ago, Brother Bob invited me to be one of the speakers at the FGBMF national convention in Dallas. When I arrived, I checked into my hotel and lay down for a minute to put my feet up before the meeting. During this time, I saw a vision. I saw the title of the organization, Full Gospel Business Men's Fellowship, appear before my eyes. Then the words *Full Gospel* disappeared, and all that remained was Business Men's Fellowship.

I asked the Lord what this meant, and He said to me, *They have lost the meaning of "Full Gospel," and this organization is in danger of losing the very thing that made them great.*

I knew that the Lord wanted me to share this word with the convention when it came my time to speak. I released the prophetic vision that God had given to me, and the response was powerful—hundreds of men came back to their first love that night, receiving a fresh mandate. Miracles, signs and wonders were clearly manifested.

After the service, Brother Bob approached me excitedly and said, "That was God!"

I was grateful that he was blessed that night, but at first I thought nothing more of the comment. Then, with bodies all over the floor in that Dallas auditorium, pressed there by the power of God, Bob and some of his associates rushed me away to tell me what he had meant by what he said. Directly before the meeting that evening, one of the leaders of the organization had raised a vote to remove the words *Full Gospel* from the official name of the group. They could not reach an agreement on this motion. Ultimately, however, Bob had said, "James Levesque is speaking tonight. He hears from God and may have a word for us. Let's just resume the vote after service!"

We compared stories further and discovered the timing lined up—right at the moment when God had given me the vision, they had been arguing over this major decision. That was the moment when Bob had advised them to wait, because they had realized that those words are more than just a name. They are a core value of who they are. Things that begin in the Holy Spirit cannot end in the flesh. This goes for our lives as well. A day is coming so very soon where the miraculous is going to be normal, everyday life.

Last year, Lyle Phillips, a well-known pastor of a church in Nashville, posted this on one of his social media accounts: "I'm not as Charismatic in my church expression as I used to be, but I'll never give up on miracles. Signs, miracles, and wonders are not a style of church. They are acts of Jesus. Miracles cause the world to marvel and the healed to give glory to God."[1] I love that, because it is an encouraging sign to me that God's Spirit is touching many today, even among those who were touched years ago. I believe it is a sign of what we will begin to experience in the days ahead—that people will begin coming back to their Holy Spirit roots.

This is just the beginning. God is going to use you powerfully in the days ahead. There is a great calling back to the things of the Spirit happening in America (and elsewhere). And guess what? You are called to lead the way. *Come on!*

Activating Your Spiritual Senses

It was a normal afternoon, and my wife and I were preparing to leave for a ministry trip. There is a couple in our church, Bill and Donna, who are like spiritual parents to me. They have stood by my side since I was in my early twenties, when very few believed in who I was. But this time, they were in need of support from me. Bill had recently been diagnosed with cancer, and my wife wanted to make them a meal before we left on our trip. So in the middle of packing and preparing for a multiweek trip, I found myself honored to drop off a meal to my good friends. Little did I know that during that visit, I would have an encounter that would transform my life.

When I arrived at their home, Bill was resting from another grueling round of treatments. I brought the food in and was delighted to have a moment to talk with Donna. I always love to talk to Donna. Although worn out from the recent battle on that day, she is someone who is always smiling and just beams the radiance of God.

We spent some time catching up. I told her about our most recent travels, and what God had been saying to me. Then I gave her an update on the church, and we spoke about our families. I also asked her about a few couples that had left the church, whom I had not had time to talk with recently. She gave a loving report, as she always does on every subject. Then I briefly expressed sadness that those couples did not finish quite the way I thought they should have in the church. This was not out of slander or with any ill motive. I was just expressing my love for and sadness about those people to a good friend. We hugged, and as I was standing next to my Jeep, I called back to Donna that Debbie and I loved her and that we would come by to see them after we returned home.

I started my Jeep down the road, and as I turned off their street, the Lord spoke very clearly to me concerning those couples that I had been expressing sadness about only moments before. Loudly and forcefully, He said, *I have not forgotten them! I am going to finish and fulfill My purposes through them!*

Immediately, I found myself repenting for anything that may have been wrong in my attitude, because, well . . . God had spoken so clearly to me. Repentance is the natural response to His voice and His goodness. Then I found myself praying for every couple I had not been able to spend time with recently. Then I transitioned away from the people whom I dearly loved and started praying for my enemies. People who have betrayed my wife and me came to my mind, and as they did, I released forgiveness, allowing my view of them to become God's view of them. I realized all over again that God's plan is just so much bigger than mine.

A New Season

Already caught up in a powerful moment with the Lord, something strange caught the corner of my eye as I was driving. This was not a vision. This was clear, as plain as day—a natural encounter. I looked up through the window of my Jeep and saw a bald eagle. Now, you may live in a region where it is a common thing to see an eagle, but I do not. I have lived in this area of Connecticut my entire life and have never seen one.

This eagle was majestic. And massive. As I looked at him, I could feel God's presence tangibly around me. I pulled over to the edge of the two-lane road as quickly as I could and looked up at the treetop where the eagle was perched, just to get a better glimpse of what I was seeing. Then the unthinkable happened. The eagle spread his wings and soared down to a branch closer to me, halfway down the tree. This was so amazing! I could see his massive wingspan, his piercing eyes. That moment, just as it was, would have been enough. It is hard even to write about it without shaking, I was so profoundly moved by this encounter. But that was not all that the Lord had in store for me that day.

Yet again, this majestic eagle opened his wings, flapped them in preparation for flight and swooped closer, this time aiming for my vehicle. On my Jeep Wrangler, there is a handle right in the center of the hood. Slowly the eagle lowered himself, and this time, he landed on the hood of my Jeep, right on that handle in the middle of it.

When recounting this story to people, I am often asked why I did not take a picture of him. If you are thinking the same thing, I will tell you what I have told others—I was scared to move my eyes! I felt the fear of the Lord all over my body. The eagle slowly tucked his wings comfortably into his sides, twisted his neck back and forth a few times, and then settled his head back, staring right at me. I felt as though God were piercing my soul. I can vividly remember the stains on his beak, the cuts and scabs on his feet. This was a totally surreal moment.

I sat trembling in my Jeep, with that eagle staring piercingly into me. It felt as if fire were swirling through my whole body. Then the Lord began to speak to me:

I am beginning a new season of prophetic destiny. This will be manifested in America and in the world. Many who have been written off by man will be restored, and for those who have been fighting long-lost battles, those battles will come to an end. History books will be written about the fulfilled promises in the days ahead. I will restore the prophetic ministry again, and a new breed of seers will arise on the earth!

I was speechless. It was hard to breathe. With tears streaming down my face, I knew something had changed. As soon as the Lord was done speaking, the eagle opened up his wings, which were longer than the width of the hood of my Jeep, and flew away. I could not drive away. I began to cry out to God, asking that He would open the eyes of a generation that we may see Him. As soon as I was able to drive again, it dawned on me— the name of the road I was sitting on was Eagle Ridge Drive.

I believe we must see the full restoration of prophetic ministry. Many have become burnt out with this "anything goes" culture of prophecy that we have today. I have seen more "words" cause damage than do good. This has not always been the case. There is a real place of visitation and encounter that will shape your life forever. We must get past the place of impressions only, and begin to believe God for accurate, life-changing words that will shape a generation.

I do not mean to discourage people from learning to move in the prophetic, and that often involves impressions. Yet clearly, there are levels in using the prophetic gifts, and this is a new season in which we should believe God that we will hear with greater clarity and insight. We need to have a thirst that leans toward accuracy and away from flaky. The gifts were made to be pursued, especially the prophetic. It is so easy, however, to become satisfied or content operating at one level.

It is important to note that angels are real and visitations do happen. But if your encounter does not leave you with heaven's residue on you, it is safe to say that it may have been you, not God. I have had visitations from angels, out-of-body experiences and incredible encounters. These moments have left me changed forever and resulted in souls being saved, in lives being transformed and, most of all, *in my life being transformed*.

Changing the Name?

People ask me all the time what the phrase *Engaging Heaven* means. They ask why this is the name of our ministry. The name came out of a two-year period of our lives when God was speaking daily, and when we gathered to seek God and see Him move, a time I will tell you more about later in this chapter.

A few years ago, I was very frustrated about what I was seeing happening in the prophetic community. A movement that started as a pure place of visitation and encounter was turning into vain imagination and flesh. This so grieved my spirit that I was seriously considering changing the name of our churches and our ministry. I did not like what I was seeing, and I did not want to be associated with it. Much of what was being spoken out "prophetically" was actually after-the-fact explanations of current events and very vague words of knowledge. Although I believe some of that can also be from God, it was obvious to me that the young people around me were beginning to operate in the flesh. And not innocent flesh either—a confident flesh.

I called a well-known prophetic voice whom I know as a good friend. He is a father in this movement and is one of the most accurate men I know. I shared with him the struggle I was having in my heart, and I asked him honestly, "Should I change the name? Should I change Engaging Heaven?"

He immediately responded, "James, I don't believe the Lord wants you to do that. You can't give up the high ground. A time is coming when God will restore the prophetic ministry, and once again, the Bride will come forth."

That was an important moment for me and for our ministry. From that point forward, we have watched God do just that.

The Eyes of Your Understanding

Ephesians 1:15–19 gives us the foundation for living in the unseen realm:

> Therefore I also, after I heard of your faith in the Lord Jesus
> and your love for all the saints, do not cease to give thanks for
> you, making mention of you in my prayers: that the God of
> our Lord Jesus Christ, the Father of glory, may give to you the
> spirit of wisdom and revelation in the knowledge of Him, the
> eyes of your understanding being enlightened; that you may
> know what is the hope of His calling, what are the riches of the
> glory of His inheritance in the saints, and what is the exceeding
> greatness of His power toward us who believe, according to the
> working of His mighty power.

Paul prays here that God would give us a spirit of wisdom and
revelation. I hope that you have prayed and are continuing to
pray this over your life daily.

Paul then asks that the "eyes of your understanding" would
be opened. We have all been gifted with a gift of sight. When
we are born again, God gives us a third eye—the eye of the
Spirit. The eye of understanding. We were created to see in the
unseen realm and live for what is going on around us spiritually.
We can get so attached to this earth that we unknowingly close
off this area of our lives. Right now, this very second, you have
an eye that God wants to open. You have the ability to see in
the spirit, and you have an eye that is open to the reality of the
supernatural realm.

According to the text, this eye also brings a great hope and
an understanding of that mighty power. The Bible is filled with
Scriptures that tell us to fix our eyes on things above. Here are
just a couple of them:

> Set your minds on things above, not on earthly things.
>
> Colossians 3:2 NIV

> For we do not wrestle against flesh and blood, but against princi-
> palities, against powers, against the rulers of the darkness of this
> age, against spiritual hosts of wickedness in the heavenly places.
>
> Ephesians 6:12

Wherever you are at this moment, there is another level of life.
There are angels, wisdom, revelation and knowledge in Christ.
We are called to live in the supernatural.

Prophecy is simple—hearing from God. That is it. Are you a
prophet? Then you hear from God more than others and have
a larger platform. It is not that complicated. People ask me all
the time what the difference is between a prophet and someone
who prophesies. The answer is simple—reason of use. Gifts are
gifts. We are all called to use them and operate in them. The
frequency of use is the difference between a prophet and someone who prophesies. The Bible says that "you can all prophesy"
(1 Corinthians 14:31), so we understand that we can all operate
in that. But those who have stretched that gift and made themselves available to operate in it prophesy more often.

While some people are called to hold the office of a prophet,
I believe that does not include as many people as we think. I
believe identifying, pressing in for and using our gifts will open
us all up to hear from God more frequently. I do not believe we
sit and wait for prophets or apostles to show up, as much as
we respect them when they do. We all have the living God in
us, and each and every one of us needs to maximize the calling
on our lives.

Years ago, the Church became so fixated on the gifts of the
Spirit, and for many years we have been so focused on having
a specific gift, that we have actually weakened the operation
of the gifts overall. We have made them singular in nature and
not a blanket of wisdom and gifts, plural. You have every gift
already in you, and God will highlight the ones you need. Whatever you make room for will dominate you. I am living proof

that you can open your ears by praying and seeking God. The Bible says in the book of Hebrews that there is a reason you may not have your eyes opened yet—reason of use:

> For though by this time you ought to be teachers, you need someone to teach you again the first principles of the oracles of God; and you have come to need milk and not solid food. For everyone who partakes only of milk is unskilled in the word of righteousness, for he is a babe. But solid food belongs to those who are of full age, that is, those who by reason of use have their senses exercised to discern both good and evil.
>
> Hebrews 5:12–14

You have spiritual senses. Everyone does. Whether or not you feel as if you are discerning good or evil, well, that is another thing. I am telling you that God will allow us to exercise those senses. How do you activate that? How do you learn to discern? *Desire.*

Desire to See

Let me tell you how it worked with me. When I was born again, I was hungry for the Word of God and wholeheartedly believed everything I read. Along with that belief came a deep desire to see and experience everything I was reading about. When I was living for myself in the world, the devil did not cut me off or limit what I could do in regard to darkness. There was never enough, and I could have all the sin I wanted. So when I encountered heaven, I wanted to learn and experience everything the Father had for me. I wanted it all.

When I was young and had just planted my first church, I was invited to attend a conference at a nearby church. This church was the center for renewal in New England, beginning in the 1990s and on into the next decade. I had no idea that this would be the church that would launch me into the ministry, and that not so very long after that night, I would be speaking at these same conferences.

My friends and I attended the morning session. There was a young man, now a good friend of mine, who was speaking about seeing in the Spirit and "going to heaven," so to speak. He spoke at length about God desiring to speak to His children and how the prophetic ministry is so valuable to the Church.

There is a reason the Bible says, "Pursue love, and desire spiritual gifts, but especially that you may prophesy" (1 Corinthians 14:1). One of the most overlooked keys in activating your spiritual senses is *desire*. We must desire the things of the Spirit. It is so important! If you do not build a hunger for the supernatural, then you will not receive the ability to see it. When you develop a thirst for the supernatural, visions are a normal occurrence. It is as natural as seeing with your own two eyes. It is just another level of the world we live in.

After that speaker's session ended, he said he wanted us to activate our senses and ask God to open our understanding. He asked that everyone close his or her eyes and just "Be." The Bible says in Psalm 46:10, "Be still, and know that I am God; I will be exalted among the nations, I will be exalted in the earth!" If you break the first part of this verse down a word at a time, it reads,

> Be still, and know that I am.
> Be still, and know that I.
> Be still, and know that.
> Be still, and know.
> Be still, and.
> Be still.
> [And finally just] Be.

Sometimes we have to just "Be." It is an essential factor in seeing the unseen realm.

The speaker asked all of us to close our eyes and "Be." No speaking in tongues, no praying out loud, no shaking—nothing.

There was not even music. As the crowd of people stood quiet and still, he simply prayed, "Holy Spirit, come. Show us what You are doing." That was it.

In that moment, you could hear people begin to sob. And I immediately saw a vision—a brook flowing down over a few rocks. It was simple, but I became unhinged. I could not believe what I was seeing. I had never "seen" before.

I turned to one of my friends near me, grabbing him and whispering loudly, "I *saw* something! I *saw* something!"

"Umm, you *should* have seen something," he replied. "That's the point!"

He shrugged me off with a laugh, but that was a day that changed my life forever. I *saw* something. I knew that if Jesus could show me one picture, He had plenty more where that came from. This happened well over fifteen years ago, but I can still remember that when I went back home, things were different. I was determined to eagerly desire the gift of hearing and seeing God.

I immediately went to many of the core leaders of our church and asked them to meet with me every day to also "see heaven." Now, I do not believe you can just go to heaven anytime you want, but I absolutely believe you can position yourself to hear from God and see Him daily in visions, in pictures and in your imagination.

For two years, every day around 5:30 a.m., this group and I came together to just "Be." There was no agenda for anything other than learning how to hear from God and activate our spiritual senses. Looking back at those moments now, it was like my Bible school. It was in that season that I learned how to hear from God and how to really make a difference in this world.

On those mornings, we would write down the words we heard or the images we saw. We filed them away and held on to them. I told everyone that if the vision they had was neutral or lined up with the Word of God, then they should write it down. (I always checked that what we saw lined up with Scripture.) If people saw something negative or anything clearly from hell, then I told them to leave it out. And every single day, we recorded what we saw.

Early on, we did not write down very much because we did not see very much. But over the course of two years, we began not only to see, but also to see with amazing clarity. God began to speak to us about events to come and about our current situations. It became a prophetic briefing for our day.

One day in particular, I remember what we all shared after worshiping and meditating for two hours. "God wants to heal a serious leg condition," someone said. (Note that I have changed the name and some other identifying details in this story to protect the individual's privacy.)

"I'm hearing the name Penny," someone else said.

"I felt that God was going to heal someone, and I saw a walker left behind," I said.

"All I saw today was a purple shirt," the last person added.

"What if this is like a prophetic puzzle, guys?" I asked excitedly. "What if God wants to heal someone named Penny who uses a walker because of her serious leg condition? And what if she has a purple shirt on so we will know that it's her?"

What a radical thought! God was going to heal someone that day through us, and we were sitting in a briefing room with the Holy Spirit. He had given us our assignment for the day, and now it was time for us to go out and do it. It was crazy to imagine such a thing.

And just like little children—although among us were a chemist, a project manager from a power plant, navy officers, managers, restaurant workers and even a homeless man—we all went out with a little piece of paper that read simply,

- Penny
- Walker

- Leg Condition
- Purple Shirt

I went to breakfast that same morning with a church friend who was like an assistant pastor to me. As we were eating, we marveled at what God had spoken to us that morning and wondered if it could actually happen. We finished our meal and left the restaurant.

As we were driving, the unthinkable happened. A mere fifty yards from where we had gathered only hours before to seek the voice of the Lord, we saw a lady using a walker. I immediately grabbed the crumpled white piece of paper from my pocket to make sure I was remembering correctly. The woman with the walker was wearing a purple shirt.

"You call her name!" I shouted to my friend.

"No, you do it!" he exclaimed back. We were both nervous.

I finally stepped out of the car and yelled, "Penny!"

She turned around.

No way! I thought. *This cannot be happening!*

My friend and I rushed over to the woman. We offered no explanation. I simply opened the note, showing her what was written on it, and she started weeping. I told her Jesus loved her so much that He had interrupted our day to send us out looking for her. She was amazed.

I reached my hand out to her. "Penny, are you ready?" She quickly grabbed my hand as I said, "In the name of Jesus, walk normally!"

In one moment of power, her years of struggling with a debilitating leg condition were over. I remember how it felt when we walked with her to the nearest dumpster and threw that walker away. She was a believer in Jesus, but not in the power of God. That changed that day. And as you read this now, she is still walking. And her walker is in a garbage dump somewhere. All because God put His hand on some crazy kid from the projects and connected me with so many people from so many different backgrounds, all for one cause. And we did not stop there.

I declare in Jesus' name that *you* will have your eyes opened today. And as you eagerly desire to see, *you will*.

Shaping Your Life with Encounters

After that simple, powerful word we received for Penny and the healing that stemmed from it, we were so stirred about what God had done. The next morning we testified to our team, and it only built more faith for more encounters. We wanted the real deal, all the time.

Aside from words and changed lives, it is really about being available. Kathryn Kuhlman used to say, "God is not looking for gold vessels or silver vessels. He is looking for yielded vessels." Being available and eager with desire is so vital. That experience with Penny on the streets of downtown New London, Connecticut, opened my eyes to the world before me. I wanted what Jesus spoke of in the book of John:

> Then Jesus answered and said to them, "Most assuredly, I say to you, the Son can do nothing of Himself, but what He sees the Father do; for whatever He does, the Son also does in like manner. For the Father loves the Son, and shows Him all things that He Himself does; and He will show Him greater works than these, that you may marvel."
>
> John 5:19–20

Encounters are real. Visions are real. Visitations are real. We cannot chase these things alone, but we must also realize that in this Christian life, we are created to explore and discover the realms of the Spirit. When you spend time in God's presence and develop a seeing eye and a hearing ear, He can move mightily.

A Hearing Heart

In 1 Kings 3:9, we see an unusual but powerful prayer of Solomon's: "Therefore give to Your servant an understanding heart to judge Your people, that I may discern between good and evil. For who is able to judge this great people of Yours?"

"Give me an understanding heart." Once as I was spending time with a well-known prophet, he turned to me and said, "James, long after I am gone, the greatest gift that you and every believer will need in the last days is a gift of discernment, to be able to discern what is good and what is evil."

At the time, I thought it was ridiculous to think that we would live in a day where good and evil are confused. Well, now we have arrived. We must have an understanding heart! It has become harder and harder to hear from God, because we are more and more distracted. The Father is looking for a group of people who will silence a thousand voices for the One.

Advancement requires purposeful positioning. Once you have positioned yourself in His presence, as you go, God will meet you. And when He does, you will not need to post about it on social media for it to garner attention. All will see it. Yet the greatest encounters in your life are not for the purpose of everyone's knowledge, at least not initially. These are powerful and solemn encounters. It is only after many, *many* years that I am finally released to share a few of my experiences with you. These encounters are precious to me. They have shaped my life and my ministry. When you create a culture of hearing God in your life and position yourself for encounter, get ready!

Pursue holiness until it hurts. Prepare for mighty encounters with His Spirit. But understand that these encounters must leave you changed. I am not talking about Twitter followers—I am talking about your words sounding different, a boldness coming upon you that you have never before known. True encounters with His presence result in lives transformed. Your family, school, workplace, the nations—all changed.

There are times when you pursue the supernatural and do not even realize what is happening. That happened to me once in Saint John, New Brunswick. Dr. Brian Simmons, who is like a father to me, saw something in me when I was praying for people on the streets and seeing souls saved. At the time, I was young and new to the ministry, but God connected me to this powerful father and friend, and he asked me to go on a trip with him to speak at a conference in the Maritimes, a region in eastern Canada.

I had never left Connecticut before, except on a few trips to local New England cities. When he asked me to speak at this conference, I was honored and, truthfully, a little freaked out. Here is why: I was so used to speaking to drug addicts and people who lived on the streets that I did not know whether or not the "church crowd" would receive me.

I often joke when I am speaking that these days, what you see is the "put-together version of me." I look nothing now like I did when I arrived in Saint John. The tattoos are permanent, so they are still there, but gone are the many piercings and the Bob Marley T-shirt I had on that day.

It goes without saying that I was out of place in that conference setting, but I had confidence in one thing—I knew how to hear the voice of God. Friend, I was spending thirteen hours in His presence each day when I first gave my life to Jesus, and then between two and five hours each day when our church went through a two-year season of asking God to open our eyes. I did not know much else but His voice. Oh, I knew that very well. I knew that His voice, visions and Word were all things in which I could put my trust. During this trip to Saint John, I would receive a major prophetic vision for the people of Canada, and I would have an encounter that would shape the next season of my ministry.

Before I recount the details of this story, let me ask you this: What would it look like today if you made room to hear God? It is not a matter of hours, but heart time that you make available. It is not the *quantity* of time, but the *quality* of time you take to hear from God and silence the world. It can be fifteen minutes, an hour, all day, whatever you feel in your heart, but the most important thing is that *you are available.* People are so desperate for a "word from God," but they are not desperate to spend time with His Spirit and cultivate a hearing ear.

I am not telling these stories about my life so you will think I am special or powerful. I would rather keep these things silent, truthfully. I am telling these stories so we can build faith together. Understand this: If God could touch an uneducated street kid from New London, Connecticut, open his ears and speak to him, He can do the same for you. Your age, race, upbringing, education and financial status—these things do not matter. God wants to open your eyes to see and your ears to hear.

When the day arrived for me to catch my plane to Saint John, I remember waking up very early. I wanted to make sure I had time to pray. I gathered with my team as usual in prayer and meditation, and God spoke. Reflecting on the moment now, I realize the Lord did not speak specifically, but everyone felt that God had something powerful to speak to those precious people gathering for the conference. I did not have a schedule for the event at that moment and did not know how much time I would be given to speak, but I knew God was calling me there and would speak through me.

I boarded a plane in Boston, with a brief layover in Montreal, and then continued on to Saint John. When we arrived in Montreal, we had to go through customs and recheck our bags. As I was approaching the next security gate from America to Canada,

I felt the power of God around me suddenly and strongly. It was as if there were a wall of power before me that I could not cross. Feeling my knees giving out, I had to stop walking. I dropped my carry-on, lifted my hands and started praying. This power was so strong that I could not remain standing. After about thirty seconds I collapsed onto the floor, right there in the airport.

I did not lose physical consciousness or awareness. This encounter felt more like being "slain in the Spirit." My body was weak, but I could still stand, a fact I realized only when a security guard rushed over to make sure I was okay. I quickly stood up and assured him I was fine. The guard, along with his co-workers who had surrounded us by then, reluctantly let me go, and as I glanced over to the Canadian side of the airport, I saw him—a massive angel stood in the corner of the room. I had never seen anything like this before. He had ice-blue wings and eyes of fire. He was wearing armor that covered his entire body. Clearly, he was a warrior, muscular and strong, standing easily thirty feet tall. He had a weathered and beaten battle helmet on his head.

I could not look away. I then noticed he was in chains, a thought that seemed strange and impossible to me because he was so obviously strong. At first, I was scared to look at him too closely because the glory was around me so powerfully. It seemed to pass too quickly and yet go on forever, and then the access to the vision ended. God had allowed me just a glimpse, and that was it. The sight I had been granted for that moment was gone. Then the Lord spoke:

> Nine years ago to the day you will speak, I released an angel of harvest and awakening in this land. This was an invitation for a Great Awakening in the Maritimes, and the opposition has now resulted in a place where I am not welcome to move.

I was shocked. I received revelation in that moment about what the Word means when it says that angels are messengers.

They partner with the Father's will, but we have to say yes. I spent the entirety of the next flight in awe of what I had seen. This was not like the prophetic words we had received with our church leadership meetings. This was a vision that could shape a nation.

When I checked in to the Saint John Trade and Convention Centre, I was beyond excited. Hundreds of people were walking around with conference badges. People were passing me by, probably believing I had wandered in off the street. Really! Someone actually walked up to me and asked if I wanted to be born again.

I found the green room, and one of Pastor Brian's assistants arrived shortly afterward. "Dr. Brian would like you to open the conference tonight," she said. "He asked me to tell you not to hold back. Just give whatever the Lord is telling you."

I realized at that moment that the Lord had given me that encounter in the airport for that very night. The moment was surreal. There were over a thousand people gathered for a conference, and I was unknown to them all. But we were all very soon to know each other by the Spirit of God and the power of His Word.

The Word Confirmed

I am reminded as I tell you this that this land has always been so dear to my heart. Through many words and mighty exploits, we have been connected to the Maritimes for life. Before this conference started, a good friend of mine who lives in New Glasgow, Nova Scotia, met me at the venue. Right now, I am imagining people seeing my friend and me filing in during the beginning of worship, and I cannot help but laugh at myself and at the whole scenario. There I was, a young thug whom nobody knew from Adam, about to get up on an international stage and release a word. God is so wild!

As worship continued, I convinced myself, *I'm just gonna release the word and sit down.* I was not the seasoned speaker I am now, and after having people try to lead me to the Lord on my way into the building, I was not even sure that what I had to say would be received. There was a brief time of announcements following worship, an even briefer introduction from Pastor Brian, and it was time. I was up.

Nervous does not begin to describe how I felt, but I went for it. I immediately shared the word that the Lord had given to me in airport customs earlier that day. I shared the entire experience in detail, and I realized that as I was speaking, the same power I had felt at the airport had come into the room. And the presence of Jesus was all that I needed. The feeling of that power, that presence, renewed my confidence. It was as though I were standing with that mighty angel staring me down once again. And I spoke with boldness and authority.

There were a few people who left the room while I was speaking. I did not think much of it in the moment, until I saw those same people walk back in toward the end of the message. Toward the end of the service, the glory of God began to sweep through the room and people ran to the altar, crying out to God. Among the crowd that came forward were two women who had left the service while I had been speaking. I noticed that one of them had a newspaper in her hands. Swiftly they approached me, looking at me with tears in their eyes.

"We want you to know that the Lord brought you to Saint John today!" one of them said. They held the newspaper up to my face. "This is the proof!"

As the conference crowd quieted to hear what was happening, I grabbed the newspaper from her hand and read the headline: "Renewal Comes to Saint John, Local Ministers Oppose." Pictured on the front of this local newspaper were five ministers looking up to the sky, arms crossed in defiance. And the kicker? It was dated *nine years to the day* prior to the very date I was speaking, just as the Lord had spoken to me.

With this powerful confirmation of the word of the Lord, the room exploded with the sound of believers crying out for awakening and transformation. To this day, it is clear that something shifted in that region forever. It has been an incredible honor over the years to go back and hear the stories of what the Lord has continued to do there.

I did not go into that weekend looking for a visitation. I did not go trying to make an encounter happen. This incredible experience was an overflow expression of what I was already doing. We have become addicted to a conference culture where speakers are like circus performers. This is not healthy for the speakers or for the people attending. May I strongly suggest that instead of getting what you need from more meetings or conferences, maybe God wants to do something in and through your heart privately? Perhaps group gatherings are a conduit of confirmation for the word you already hold in your heart daily.

With well over a million miles traveled since that first conference, not a thing has changed for me in this respect. I go to a region, ask the Father to show me what He is doing and then He speaks. It is that simple and that powerful. That weekend in Saint John opened my eyes to many things. That experience showed me the power of an encounter. It showed me that we must make ourselves available to God for what He wants to do. It taught me that we must shape our world with encounters, and that the touch of God is our everything. His presence is all we need.

Preparing for Encounter

We do not encounter God at will. It is not something we have control over. God is always speaking, however, and we must do two crucial things to prepare for more encounters: Make time for God and pray, pray, pray.

Making time is simple. We must pull ourselves away from distractions and allow the Holy Spirit to move and do what He wants to do. I believe the lack of true prophets on this earth is connected to a lack of devotion. We have come as far as we can with our current level of surrender. The spiritual climate of the Church reminds me so much of 1 Samuel 3:1–10:

> Now the boy Samuel ministered to the LORD before Eli. And the word of the LORD was rare in those days; there was no widespread revelation. And it came to pass at that time, while Eli was lying down in his place, and when his eyes had begun to grow so dim that he could not see, and before the lamp of God went out in the tabernacle of the LORD where the ark of God was, and while Samuel was lying down, that the LORD called Samuel. And he answered, "Here I am!" So he ran to Eli and said, "Here I am, for you called me."
>
> And he said, "I did not call; lie down again." And he went and lay down.
>
> Then the LORD called yet again, "Samuel!"
>
> So Samuel arose and went to Eli, and said, "Here I am, for you called me." He answered, "I did not call, my son; lie down again." (Now Samuel did not yet know the LORD, nor was the word of the LORD yet revealed to him.)
>
> And the LORD called Samuel again the third time. So he arose and went to Eli, and said, "Here I am, for you did call me."
>
> Then Eli perceived that the Lord had called the boy. Therefore Eli said to Samuel, "Go, lie down; and it shall be, if He calls you, that you must say, 'Speak, LORD, for Your servant hears.'" So Samuel went and lay down in his place.
>
> Now the LORD came and stood and called as at other times, "Samuel! Samuel!"
>
> And Samuel answered, "Speak, for Your servant hears."

Notice how verse 1 says that "the word of the LORD was rare in those days." Let me ask you a question: Was His word rare because He was not speaking? Or was it because the people were not listening? Which one was it?

Eli was not only physically blind, but also spiritually blind, making excuses for the sin of his sons, which resulted in a lack of God's word on the earth. The word of the Lord is all about positioning. The Father longs to speak to us, so much so that He bypassed Eli in this instance. It was unusual for God to bypass the high priest, yet instead He spoke to Samuel. The Lord saw that Samuel was available, making time in the place of His presence, and He spoke. And Eli was not happy about it.

As you read in the Scripture passage, Eli told Samuel many times to go lie back down. This is the equivalent of saying, "Look, kid, it's not your time yet!" But that could not have been further from the truth. The third time the Lord called out to Samuel, Eli accepted what was happening and instructed Samuel about what to say when the Lord spoke again. That was not an easy task for Eli, because ultimately, it meant his demise. But Eli knew that when the Lord speaks, you must listen.

We find ourselves in a similar situation today. The word of the Lord is rare. What is going to change that? You and I making room to hear God, living holy and realizing that we were made for the supernatural!

Radical Prayer

Prayer and worship play a vital role in outpouring. We have to find the proper place of prayer, holding on to promises and not letting go. Prayer does not change God's mind; prayer changes us. Prayer changes our circumstances. We must understand the Father's will so that we can carry it out on this earth.

We find two different words in Scripture that are translated into the word *will*. God has a concrete *will*, an unmovable agenda that we can never touch. His will is happening no matter what. No one gets a say in that. Then there is another word for will that also translates as *desire*. It is still the will of God, but in many cases, God chooses to live within the limitations of *our obedience* (our desire).

It is the Father's will that none should perish: "The Lord is not slack concerning His promise, as some count slackness, but is longsuffering toward us, not willing that any should perish but that all should come to repentance" (2 Peter 3:9). But do people still perish? Sadly, yes. That outcome does not fall solely on God's side of the contract. Much of that lies on the back of believers' failure to carry out their commission to preach, proclaim and declare.

How do we accomplish God's will on this earth? By understanding His promises, waiting and praying. These are the actions that position us for encounter. From the place of encounter, we will shake this world for God. Just as in the Upper Room, where one encounter changed eternity, receive a fresh baptism and transform your family and your region.

You have heard just a few key pieces of my story—moments of my life that changed me forever and left me burning for more. It is my desire that you would begin to make room again for Jesus. Even now, I give you permission to put this book down and get in God's presence. Worship Him—just "Be."

I believe that when you do that, you will be amazed at what you see. And do not doubt that all the questions you have right now, all the things you have wrestled with, the drama and trauma, will end. The answers you need cannot be found in worry, people, success or perfect circumstances. The answers are waiting for you in His presence. I give you permission to go. Today marks the beginning of transformation in your life. Go. He is waiting!

Believing Outpouring Can Continue

When we purchased our historic building, I thought it was a sign. We were a young, radical group believing for another Great Awakening, and we were about to purchase one of the most historic sites in America. This was a building used during the Great Awakening era. Our region saw thousands gathered there, even though there was not enough room, to hear George Whitefield, Jonathan Edwards, David Brainerd and many other early preachers from the Great Awakening, on the very land we were standing on. And there we were, taking the baton.

Not many are interested in what used to be, but I have always taken a great interest in the past. It is not that I want to replicate exactly what happened long ago. I know that God will move differently today. Yet what happened then and what we hope for now will all come to the same end—outpouring and awakening. It is vitally important for believers to understand prophetic history. Looking at the marks and measures of what

God has done before can motivate us to pray in agreement and believe for a greater version to happen in the here and now.

When our purchase of the building was complete, I was given a book that documented the entirety of the church's history, starting with when it was the First Church of Christ, New London, Connecticut. The book recounts all the men who pastored in the building, dating back to the 1700s. As I was thumbing through the pages, I came across three chapters labeled "The Great Awakening." I found these to be an inspiration and an insight into what it would look like today if God moved powerfully again.[1]

As I read, I was stirred about the miracles God had done in times past. There was one testimony of a man who stood up in the middle of a meeting and cursed God and the preacher. The crowd was left aghast as the man angrily stormed out of the building. When he reached the outside steps, a lightning bolt flashed from heaven and struck him dead. You cannot make this kind of thing up! The fear of the Lord was so strong in that day.

Toward the end of the last chapter about the Great Awakening, the book mentioned the growth and some of the fruit of the Awakening. As I read about its effects, I thought about how the Great Awakening lasted only a few decades, and then it basically was brought to naught. You read that right—despite its amazing effects, it soon came to an end. The Lord spoke this to me as I finished that last chapter: *I never desire the move of My Spirit to end. Man gets in the way.*

What a humbling revelation. We have had many amazing moves of God in America and around the earth, and to think, none of them were supposed to end. Wrapping our minds around an outpouring of His Spirit that does not end is difficult. What about a breakthrough? What about a healing? I want you to think about the greatest experiences with the Lord that you have ever had. Now imagine those encounters never ending. This is possible—we *can* live in a constant realm of breakthrough and transformation.

The Mountaintop

Shortly after I was saved I was really on fire for God, loving the Holy Spirit, hungry for His Word and believing for breakthrough and regional transformation. I mentioned earlier that the church I was attending at the time had a "Holy Spirit Night" every Saturday night, with an extended time for prayer and a focus on the baptism of the Holy Spirit. I loved those services. God spoke to me and touched me many times while I attended.

On one particular evening, the pastor called on me to pray. I remember praying with such passion and power as we all stood in a circle together. Praying out loud in front of people was very new to me, yet despite my immaturity, God was faithful and used me. He always gave me the words to speak. While I was praying, I began to travail for awakening, and it was such a push of power. It was one of the times I remember feeling as if we were going to a new level just through prayer.

When the evening was over, the pastor closed in prayer and dismissed the service. We began to file out of the building, and as we did, one of the deacons of the church approached me. He was a tall, towering guy with a long beard. He looked like Moses, so anything he said was pretty intimidating.

This deacon leaned over, looking down on me, and said, "Powerful prayer, young man. But I need to tell you that right now, you're on the mountaintop, and you can't always live on the mountaintop. You will have valleys and trials, and you won't always be excited like this."

I obviously do not agree with this mentality now, and even as a less-experienced believer at the time, I was not buying it. People who do not believe that we can live every day in revival just have not experienced enough of God. As a matter of fact, the Bible says in the book of James,

> Consider it pure joy, my brothers and sisters, whenever you face trials of many kinds, because you know that the testing of your faith produces perseverance. Let perseverance finish its work so that you may be mature and complete, not lacking anything.
>
> James 1:2–4 NIV

Trials can actually set you up *never to lack*. So often, people speak out of their own barrenness rather than out of the Word of God. We cannot allow the lack we have experienced in the past to be the measuring stick of our expectations for the future.

It was Bill Johnson who once said, "Bible study without Bible experience is pointless." I agree wholeheartedly. We were not created to be robots, serving God without emotion or feeling. When I was living for the devil, there was no threshold for sin. I could have as much destruction as I wanted. When I gave my heart to Jesus, I began to devour the Word of God, and I wanted everything I read about. I wanted to taste and see.

Much of today's Christianity is a smoke-and-mirror show that does not provide a personal experience, or it is dead faith that does not produce results but still demands that you serve blindly. Do not listen to anyone who tells you that you are chasing an experience or a feeling. If I had listened to those people, I would never have traveled over a million miles seeing signs and wonders around the world. I would not ever have planted churches. It is so important that we do not let people who have given up on their pursuits talk us out of ours.

There are two principles in your life that will qualify you continually for never-ending awakening and a life of personal revival: prayer and surrender.

What You Are Carrying

I am going to say something, but I do not want you to be offended. (Truthfully, if you have made it this far, you are a friend and a world-changer who won't be offended.) Here it is: *You do not matter.*

I know, I know. Tough to hear, tough to accept. If it helps, *I do not matter, either.*

As far as God loving you and me and Jesus dying for us, yes, we matter. As far as His miracle power flowing through our lives and the Father being revealed through us, *the less of us, the better.* We are only vessels. And what makes a vessel valuable is what is inside it, not the vessel itself.

It is kind of like a pizza box. A pizza box may not seem to have value. When it is sitting empty on your counter or in your recycling bin, no one pays attention to it. It is a cardboard box. Just a few hours before, however, everyone lined up around your counter for that box because of what was in it. The value of the pizza box rises when there is actual pizza in it.

It is the same thing with empty vessels. Look at 2 Kings 4:1–3:

> A certain woman of the wives of the sons of the prophets cried out to Elisha, saying, "Your servant my husband is dead, and you know that your servant feared the LORD. And the creditor is coming to take my two sons to be his slaves."
>
> So Elisha said to her, "What shall I do for you? Tell me, what do you have in the house?" And she said, "Your maidservant has nothing in the house but a jar of oil."
>
> Then he said, "Go, borrow vessels from everywhere, from all your neighbors—empty vessels; do not gather just a few."

The power was not in the many vessels, but in the oil. We must understand that oil is never an issue. God has unlimited oil, unlimited anointing power, available for you. That never changes. When God thinks about using you powerfully in the days ahead,

He knows that the power and authority for the things you will do have already been given to you. It has been the plan of the Father from the beginning that you and I would be carriers of the glory. We were made to reflect Jesus and shine His glory on this earth.

Let's focus on the vessels in this story. The prophet told the widow to get vessels, and not just a few. It is the vessels that determine how much oil we will carry. We are all vessels. The Bible says that every great house contains vessels for the use of the house: "But in a great house there are not only vessels of gold and silver, but also of wood and clay, some for honor and some for dishonor" (2 Timothy 2:20).

It is important to understand that it is still a great house, no matter what vessels it contains. Whether it is your church, your home, your nation or whatever it may be, it is still great. And in this great house, there are vessels of honor and dishonor. We make the decision whether we are considered a vessel of honor, fit for the Master's use. We must become a vessel that is shiny and clean on the inside, for the continued use of the Master.

The oil did not stop until the vessels stopped coming. It was not the oil that ran dry, but the vessels that ran out. We can hold back the move of God on this earth by not being available vessels for the outpouring oil.

What Defiles You?

You and I are vessels fit for the Master's use. The more we desire to live cleanly and not defile our vessel, the more power and glory can pour out from us. Jesus explained that it is the things that reside within us that defile us, not our external appearance:

> When He had called the multitude to Himself, He said to them, "Hear and understand: Not what goes into the mouth defiles a man; but what comes out of the mouth, this defiles a man."
>
> Matthew 15:10–11

This was hard for some to understand (and still is today), so when Jesus was questioned about this statement, He explained it further:

> So Jesus said, "Are you also still without understanding? Do you not yet understand that whatever enters the mouth goes into the stomach and is eliminated? But those things which proceed out of the mouth come from the heart, and they defile a man. For out of the heart proceed evil thoughts, murders, adulteries, fornications, thefts, false witness, blasphemies. These are the things which defile a man, but to eat with unwashed hands does not defile a man."
>
> Matthew 15:16–20

Only that which is in our hearts can truly defile us. Why are Christians so concerned with the outside of the cup? The way you look will never determine your holiness. We know this. Every Sunday around the world, people go to church dressed in their best but dying on the inside. It is the greatest of deceptions to focus only on the outer appearance, to be so vain that our presentation is greater than our power. We have settled for a form of power, not the real thing.

Hear me: There is unlimited oil available for every vessel! We must remain empty of this world and the knowledge of this world, and stay filled with the power and presence of God. The Pharisees prayed loudly in the streets and synagogues so that people would notice them, and Jesus said they had received their reward in full. We must live pure in our intentions and devotion to Christ, so that we do not let unhealthy ambition cause us to settle for a reward that is empty.

Recently, my mom has been in a cleaning mode. I cannot decide if this is just what people do when they get older and retire or not, but she is so focused on "cleaning out." And as she has been cleaning, she has discovered old photos, baby toys, collectibles and other mementos that have meaning to us. She gave me some of these items just a few days ago. Since we did not have a lot of money or possessions in those early days, I was shocked that my mom even had any photos of that time. It was so nice to see some of the memories captured on film, and I tucked the photos into a pocket in my Jeep and went on with my day.

Later that day, at dinner, an advertisement popped up on one of my social media accounts. It was for a "mom blog," and I just could not help but laugh at the blogger's photos. Everything was staged—an absolutely pristine and perfect home, the mom's makeup perfectly applied, studio-quality lighting, her child playing quietly with only one toy in a corner.

I recalled the photos my mother had given me earlier that day, so I grabbed them out of my Jeep. Oh, friend, I laughed at the comparison! Our home was messy, with ashtrays out on the coffee table, and I was wearing dirty clothes. The contrast was astonishing and, honestly, so laughable. The projection of what motherhood should look like today is just unattainable, and there are millions of mothers scrolling through these posts, grieving the fact that they will never live up to an image that is not even reality.

Unfortunately, many of us live our Christian lives similarly— totally staged and controlled, covering up filth and unruliness behind the production. Unlike the perfect and totally unrealistic image projected of American motherhood, however, you and I actually *can* attain a level of spiritual awakening that demonstrates "on earth as it is in heaven" in our lives, where we "prove what is that good and acceptable and perfect will of God" (Romans 12:2). It is never too good to be true. When we keep the inside of the vessel clean, we can be filled with all the fullness of God.

Awakening Prayer

Prayer, although often misunderstood, absolutely changes things. It is our connection to God. Prayer is not about changing God's mind. It is about changing our lives and our circumstances. God's mind has been made up, but our story is still unfolding. We have to look at every promise in the Bible as a contract, and God honors His contracts.

We recently moved into a new home to be closer to the church locations. If you have ever moved even once, you understand that this is quite a process. When we went to the closing of our home, I noticed a stack of papers that I had to sign that seemed as if it were two feet tall. I was taken aback by it, and I asked, "What happened? A few years ago we signed documents for a house, and it was only half the size of this stack!"

The people present for the closing laughed and told me that more liabilities mean more waivers. What they meant was that the more people who sue or find ways to break agreements, the more waivers have to be added. As I looked at the stack, I thanked God that He is always good on His Word. People may break promises, but He never will.

God guarantees that He will keep His promises. He cannot, however, guarantee your choices. His promises are conditional on us saying yes. Prayer helps us apprehend these promises and stay in the will of God.

God told a whole generation that they were going to a land flowing with milk and honey. He told *over a million people* that they were being released from bondage and would receive the Promised Land. And how many made it in the end? *Two people.*

Their journey into the Promised Land should have taken eleven days but ended up taking forty years. Unbelief is the only reason it took that long. It was *never* God's will for 999,998 to miss it. They collectively chose that path. Psalm 78:12–20 explains exactly what happened:

Marvelous things He did in the sight of their fathers, in the land of Egypt, in the field of Zoan. He divided the sea and caused them to pass through; and He made the waters stand up like a heap. In the daytime also He led them with the cloud, and all the night with a light of fire. He split the rocks in the wilderness, and gave them drink in abundance like the depths. He also brought streams out of the rock, and caused waters to run down like rivers.

But they sinned even more against Him by rebelling against the Most High in the wilderness. And they tested God in their heart by asking for the food of their fancy. Yes, they spoke against God: They said, "Can God prepare a table in the wilderness? Behold, He struck the rock, so that the waters gushed out, and the streams overflowed. Can He give bread also? Can He provide meat for His people?"

The Israelites questioned God continually about His promise. Prayer adjusts our thinking so that we will not do that. We must always be possessed with a promise and allow all that God said to be in the forefront of our minds. Prayer keeps this prioritized. It keeps first things first.

In a book first released in the 1970s called *Destined for the Throne*, the author, Paul Billheimer, said something so controversial, yet so powerful: "Prayer is our training in reigning for eternity."[2] This is so true. Our lives are about engaging heaven for all that God has and pulling those promises down to this earth. Prayer does just that.

Staying in Labor

In the book of Galatians, Paul was addressing some carnal aspects of the church in Galatia. They were taking liberty and turning it into a religious system, appealing to the world. This burdened Paul: "My little children, for whom I labor in birth again until Christ is formed in you, I would like to be present with you now and to change my tone; for I have doubts about you" (Galatians 4:19–20).

171

Paul likens prayer to labor. The pain of labor is not felt by anyone but the one who is in labor. When we labor in prayer, nobody sees it, but once the promise is produced, everyone recognizes it. Think about the days and months and years ahead in your Christian walk, and get excited. As you think about what God desires to do in your life, get excited. You are birthing something. That is why you have been in pain at times. Something is being formed in you, a child of promise.

I labor for outpouring in America. I labor for outpouring in New England. I labor for the nations to experience a global outpouring.

I challenge you to let this book be a match that ignites your faith. I challenge you to desire holiness. I challenge you to dust off the prayer journals and write again. Clean out a room in your house for prayer again. I encourage you to begin to share your faith again. I charge you to find a Holy Spirit community of like-minded believers to share your life with. And give! Give your life to see the fullness of God established on this earth.

I hope to meet you someday. But if that never happens, I know that one day in heaven, I will hear about all that God has done in and through you. *Come on!*

Notes

Principle 1 Learning to Receive

1. Annie Hawks and Robert Lowry, "I Need Thee Every Hour," 1872, hymn in the public domain, https://www.umcdiscipleship.org/resources/history-of-hymns-i-need-thee-every-hour.

2. C. Michael Hawn, "History of Hymns: 'I Need Thee Every Hour,'" *Discipleship Ministries* (The United Methodist Church), 2018, https://www.umcdiscipleship.org/resources/history-of-hymns-i-need-thee-every-hour.

Principle 3 Walking in Boldness

1. Norman P. Grubb, *C .T. Studd, Cricketer & Pioneer* (Fort Washington, Penn.: Christian Literature Crusade, 1982) 145.

Principle 7 Living Surrendered

1. Shaun Usher, ed., "The other guy just blinked," *Letters of Note*, January 20, 2012, http://www.lettersofnote.com/2012/01/other-guy-just-blinked.html.

2. Rachid Haoues, "30 Years Ago Today, Coca-Cola Made Its Worst Mistake," *CBS News*, April 23, 2015, https://www.cbsnews.com/news/30-years-ago-today-coca-cola-new-coke-failure/.

Principle 8 Living a Life That Worships

1. *Merriam-Webster Unabridged*, s.v. "Worship," http://unabridged.merriam-webster.com/unabridged/worship.

2. Jason Upton (@Jason_Upton), Twitter, July 25, 2018, https://twitter.com/Jason_Upton/status/1022310879910666240.

Principle 9 Never Forgetting the Purpose

1. Lyle Phillips (@lylebphillips), Twitter, August 13, 2018, https://twitter.com/lylebphillips/status/1029124200194289667.

Principle 12 Believing Outpouring Can Continue

1. See S. Leroy Blake, *The Later History of the First Church of Christ, New London, Conn.* (New London: Press of the Day Publishing Company, 1900). This book is available to read or download free online, for example on the Internet Archive, https://archive.org/details/laterhistoryoffi00blak/page/n5.

2. Paul E. Billheimer, *Destined for the Throne: How Spiritual Warfare Prepares the Bride of Christ for Her Eternal Destiny*, rev. ed. (Minneapolis: Bethany House, 1996), 44.

James Levesque serves as a pastor, international speaker, author and church planter. He is considered a young, emerging apostolic voice in America and the nations. His heart is to see awakening and revival throughout America and around the rest of the world.

Along with traveling, James and his wife, Debbie, pastor and lead various Engaging Heaven Churches throughout New England. Lives are transformed weekly through services, outreaches, classes, media and conferences. James is also host of the *Engaging Heaven Today* podcast, a weekday devotional focused on Spirit-filled living.

James and Debbie (who is from Vancouver, British Columbia) have been married for over eleven years and have three beautiful children, Isaac, Luke and Amayah. They live in a dreamy coastal New England town called Madison, Connecticut. When not on the road, they enjoy life in New England. They love hosting parties and spending time with family and friends. They also love all things football and coffee.

To find out more about James and his ministry, visit engagingheaven.com, or listen to his daily podcast, *Engaging Heaven Today*. To invite James to speak, contact engagingheaven @gmail.com. You can also keep up with him online:

Facebook: www.facebook.com/EngagingHeavenToday/
Twitter and Instagram: @James_Levesque